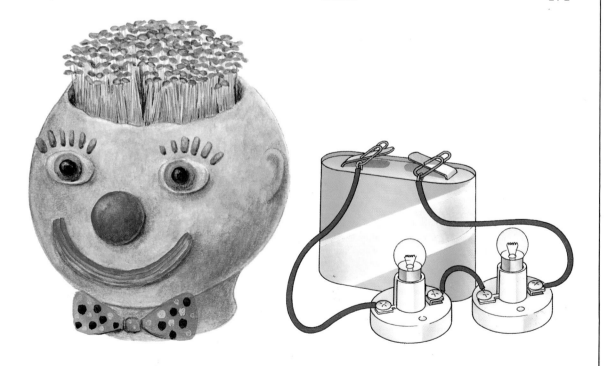

ABOUT THIS BOOK

This book is all about discovering how and why things happen in the world around you. It takes a closer look at ordinary objects, such as bread, candles, feathers and balloons. It also looks at activities, from cooking and painting to growing bulbs or flying kites. The investigations will help you to understand the importance of simple scientific ideas in your everyday life.

Do not worry if the results of your investigations are not the same as those in the book. Science is all about making new discoveries. It is a good idea to repeat the investigations to check your results and see if you can work out why your results might be different.

Here are some ideas for the kinds of simple materials used in the investigations in this book. You could keep them in a special box, so that they are easy to find.

scissors, cardboard, modelling clay, paints and brushes, colouring pencils, sticky tape or glue, old boxes or plastic cartons, empty plastic bottles and bowls, torches, cotton reels, aluminium foil, balsa wood, string, cloth, balloons, knitting needles, elastic bands, paper clips, newspaper, straws, pins, spoons, batteries, bulbs, wires, magnets.

Hints for Investigations

* Before you start, read through the instructions carefully and collect all the materials you need.
* Put on some old clothes or wear an apron or an overall.
* Clear a space to work on and cover the surface with newspaper or an old cloth.
* Take care when cutting things and ask an adult to help you with any difficult or dangerous steps.
* When you have finished, clear up any mess you have made and wash your hands.

Air and Flight

Why do you need air to survive? Why do things go rusty?
What makes food sometimes go mouldy? Why do we use
baking powder in cooking? Why does a hot-air balloon rise
up into the air? How does a barometer work? How does an
aeroplane take off and fly through the air? Why do
dandelion seeds have parachutes? Why are birds such
efficient flying machines?

This section will help you to discover the answers to these
questions and has lots of ideas for ways to investigate air
and flight.

 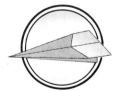

In this section, you can discover why we need air to survive, how the weather is caused by moving air and how machines and animals fly through the air.

The section is divided into six different topics. Look out for the big headings with a circle at each end – like the one at the top of this page.

Pages 12–19

Air All Around

Air everyday; breathing air; burning; rusting; air in cooking.

Pages 20–23

Warm Air, Cold Air

Hot-air balloons; convection currents.

Pages 24–27

Air Pushes Back

Compressed air; air pressure; siphons; hovercraft.

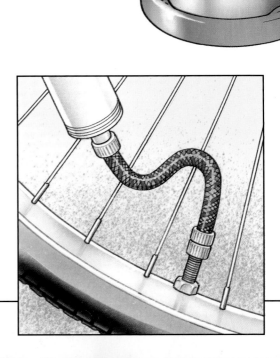

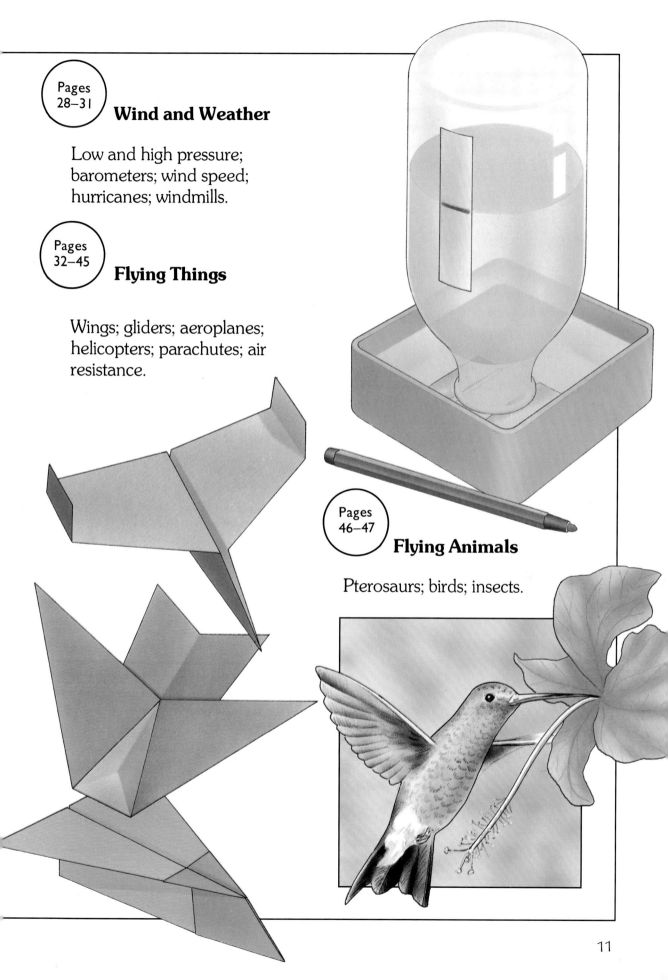

AIR ALL AROUND

Air is everywhere. It fills the space all around you. It is inside plants and animals, mugs and saucepans, bicycle tyres and balloons. Soil and water also contain air. Because we cannot see, smell or taste air, we often forget that it is there. The best way to investigate air is to look at what it does to things around you.

The pictures along the bottom of these two pages will give you some ideas. How many more examples can you think of? Make up a story or write a poem about how air affects your life.

Bubbles of air in a fizzy drink

▶ When air moves from place to place, we call it the wind. A windy day is a good time to fly a kite. The force of the wind pushes the kite up into the sky.

Blowing up a balloon

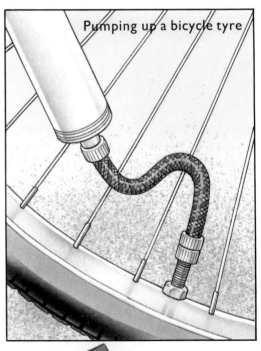
Pumping up a bicycle tyre

12

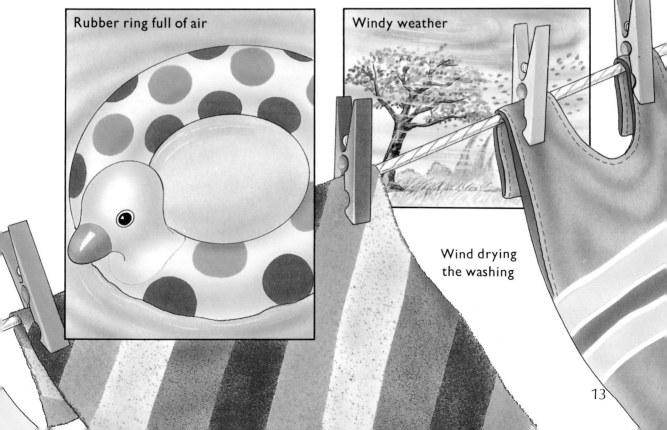

Rubber ring full of air

Windy weather

Wind drying
the washing

13

Breath Power

Why do you need air? When you breathe in, air is sucked into your lungs. In your lungs, one of the gases in the air – called oxygen – passes into your blood. The blood carries oxygen to every part of the body. You need oxygen to release the energy stored in your food. Without oxygen, you could not survive. All plants and animals need the oxygen in the air to stay alive.

Count how many times you breathe in during one minute. Then run on the spot or up and down stairs for one minute and count again. Repeat the same test after standing still for five minutes or after cycling or swimming. Compare all your results.

You could also feel your pulse before and after taking exercise. To do this, place a finger on the side of your neck or on the inside of your wrist. Your pulse tells you how fast your heart is beating. When you exercise, you need more oxygen, so you breathe faster. The heart beats faster to pump your blood, and the oxygen it carries, around the body.

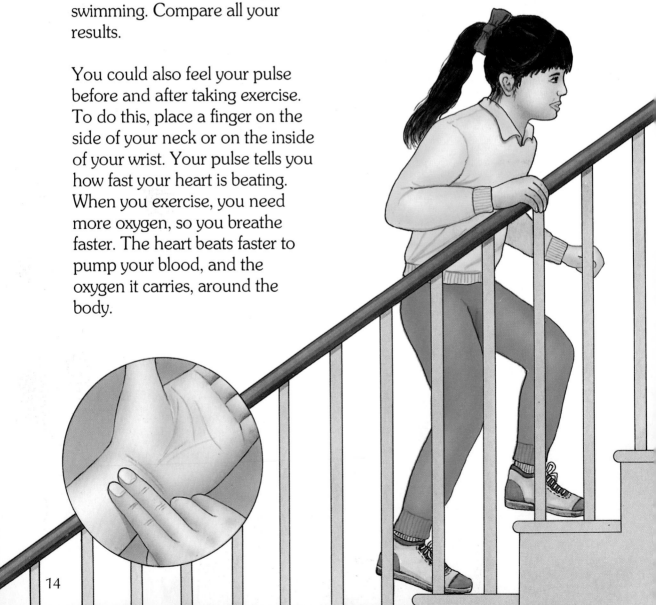

How big are your lungs?

This experiment will show the amount of air your lungs hold.

1. Fill the bowl half full of water.
2. Fill the large bottle with water. Stick tape on one side.
3. Hold the bottle over the bowl, put your hand over the neck and carefully turn the bottle upside down. Hold the neck of the bottle under the water. Mark the water level on the tape.
4. Ask a friend to hold the bottle upright and push one end of the plastic tubing into the neck of the bottle.
5. Take a deep breath and blow as hard as you can down the tubing.
6. Mark the level of the water in the bottle when you have finished.
7. Turn the bottle up the right way again. Use the measuring jug or cylinder to pour water into the bottle up to the first mark you made on the side. The amount of water you add is roughly the same as the amount of air in your lungs. It is called your lung capacity.
8. Repeat the test after taking an ordinary breath. How much air do you breathe out this time? Compare your lung capacity with your friends'.

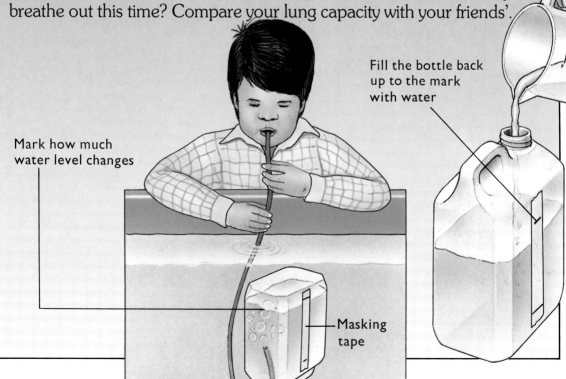

Fill the bottle back up to the mark with water

Mark how much water level changes

Masking tape

Candles and Burning

Things need oxygen in the air to burn. Prove this with candles.

Fix two night-light candles firmly to saucers with modelling clay. Ask an adult to light the candles and put a small jar over one of them. How long do they burn?

What happens

The candle under the jar soon goes out because it uses up all the oxygen. The other candle has lots of oxygen around it, so it burns for longer. Try this test with a larger jar. How long does the candle stay alight this time?

▼ Have you ever noticed flaky brown or red patches on old cars? When iron is left in damp air, it joins with oxygen in the air to form a red powder, which we call rust. Without oxygen, iron will not rust.

Make a Fruit Salad

You will need:
half a lemon, a lemon squeezer, a bowl, a saucer, a chopping board and knife, a spoon, fresh fruit, plastic wrap.

1. Squeeze the juice from the lemon and pour it into the bowl.
2. Ask an adult to help you slice up the fruit.
3. Put one slice of each fruit in the saucer, the rest in the bowl.
4. Use the spoon to cover the fruit in the bowl with lemon juice.
5. Cover the bowl with plastic wrap and put it in the refrigerator. Leave the saucer of fruit out in the air. Which fruit goes brown?

What happens

The oxygen in the air reacts with the fruit and chemical changes make the fruit in the saucer change colour. But the acid in the lemon juice helps to stop this chemical change happening to the fruit in the bowl.

Mouldy food

Leave some boiled potato, orange peel, cheese and stale bread in old saucers on a windowsill. Sprinkle each with water. Which food goes mouldy first? What colour is the mould?

Floating in the air are the tiny spores of a group of fungi called moulds. If these spores land on food, they start to feed and produce more spores. This makes the food turn mouldy.

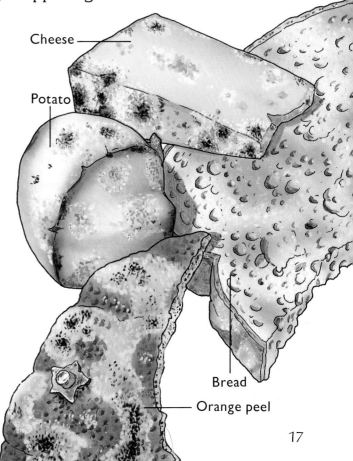

Cheese

Potato

Bread

Orange peel

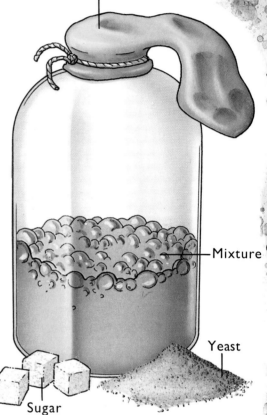

Tie the balloon onto the top

Bubbles in Bread

Use the carbon dioxide given off by yeast to blow up a balloon.

1. Half fill a small jar with warm water and add four sugar cubes.
2. Use the spoon to stir the water until the sugar disappears.
3. Pour the sugary water into the tall bottle.
4. Mix one teaspoon of the yeast with a little water.
5. Add this mixture to the bottle.
6. Use the string to tie the balloon over the neck of the bottle. Leave the bottle in a warm place.

Mixture

Yeast

Sugar

What happens

The yeast feeds on the sugar, grows and gives off carbon dioxide gas. This gas will blow up the balloon. It also makes air holes in bread.

Making Cakes

If you make a cake with plain flour, you need to add baking powder to make the cake light and full of air. Baking powder, like yeast, gives off bubbles of carbon dioxide gas if mixed with water and heated.

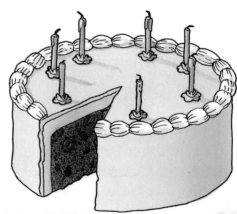

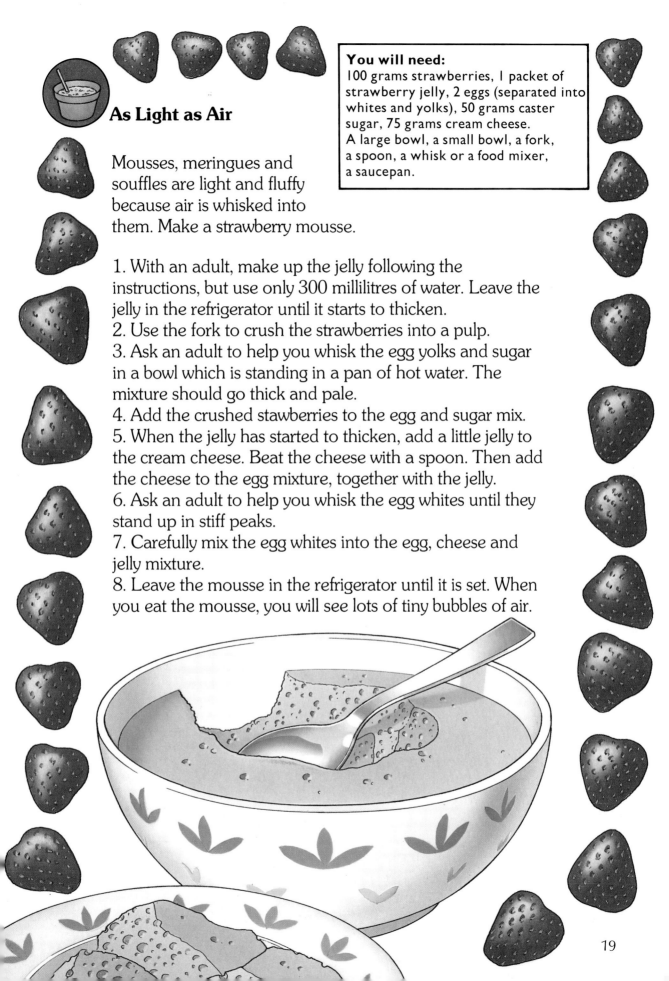

As Light as Air

You will need:
100 grams strawberries, 1 packet of strawberry jelly, 2 eggs (separated into whites and yolks), 50 grams caster sugar, 75 grams cream cheese.
A large bowl, a small bowl, a fork, a spoon, a whisk or a food mixer, a saucepan.

Mousses, meringues and souffles are light and fluffy because air is whisked into them. Make a strawberry mousse.

1. With an adult, make up the jelly following the instructions, but use only 300 millilitres of water. Leave the jelly in the refrigerator until it starts to thicken.
2. Use the fork to crush the strawberries into a pulp.
3. Ask an adult to help you whisk the egg yolks and sugar in a bowl which is standing in a pan of hot water. The mixture should go thick and pale.
4. Add the crushed stawberries to the egg and sugar mix.
5. When the jelly has started to thicken, add a little jelly to the cream cheese. Beat the cheese with a spoon. Then add the cheese to the egg mixture, together with the jelly.
6. Ask an adult to help you whisk the egg whites until they stand up in stiff peaks.
7. Carefully mix the egg whites into the egg, cheese and jelly mixture.
8. Leave the mousse in the refrigerator until it is set. When you eat the mousse, you will see lots of tiny bubbles of air.

WARM AIR, COLD AIR

Have you ever watched a bonfire? Sparks from the fire are carried upwards by warm air rising from the fire. As air gets warmer, the particles of which it is made spread out. This makes the air lighter or less dense so it rises upwards. As air cools, it becomes heavier or more dense and sinks downwards again. When heat is carried by the air itself, the process is called convection.

 Falling feathers

Let go of a small feather in different places around a room. Can you find any places where the feather will rise? (A warm radiator is a good place to try.) How high does the feather rise? How long is it in the air?

Bubbles, talcum powder or flour will also help you to detect rising hot air currents.

▲ Air inside a hot-air balloon is heated by a gas flame below the balloon. The hot air inside the balloon is lighter or less dense than the cooler air outside the balloon. As the hot air rises, it carries the balloon upwards. When the gas flame is turned down, the air cools and the balloon sinks back to the ground.

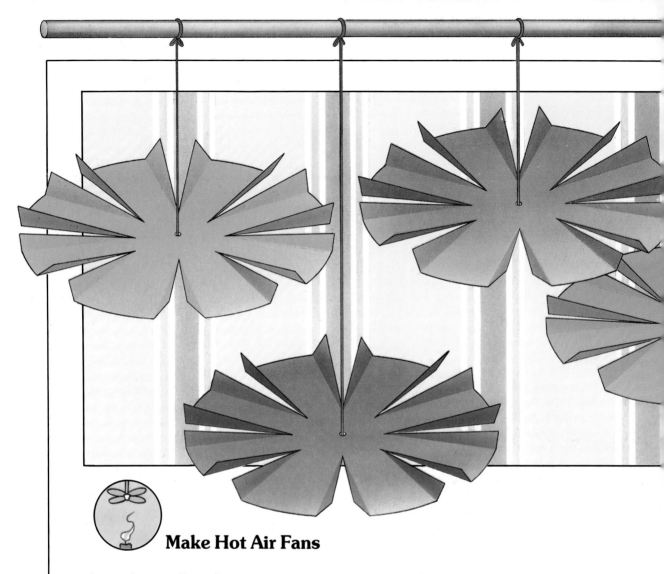

Make Hot Air Fans

These fans will twirl around in rising currents of warm air.

You will need:
coloured paper, a mug or jar, a pencil, a ruler, scissors, thread, tape, a thin stick or piece of dowel.

1. On the coloured paper, draw several circles by tracing around the outside of the mug or jar. Make each circle about 5 centimetres across.
2. Cut out the circles.
3. Fold each circle in half, then in half again and in half a third time.
4. Open out the circles. You should have eight fold lines in each circle.
5. On each fold line, measure 3.5 centimetres from the edge and put a pencil mark.
6. Cut along each fold line up to the pencil dot.
7. Bend up the cut edges, so that each bends the same way.

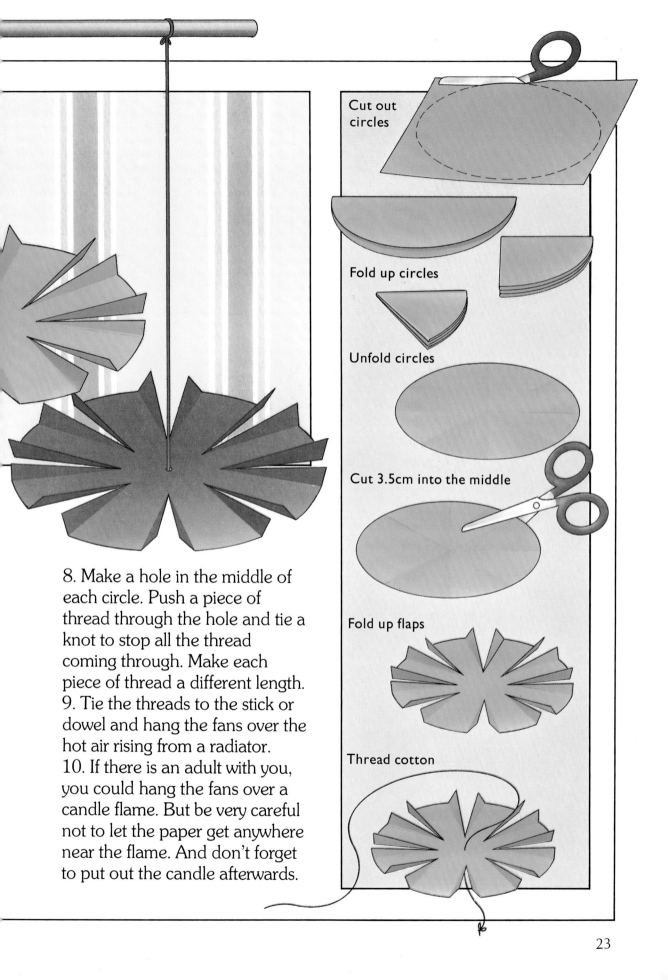

Cut out
circles

Fold up circles

Unfold circles

Cut 3.5cm into the middle

Fold up flaps

Thread cotton

8. Make a hole in the middle of
each circle. Push a piece of
thread through the hole and tie a
knot to stop all the thread
coming through. Make each
piece of thread a different length.
9. Tie the threads to the stick or
dowel and hang the fans over the
hot air rising from a radiator.
10. If there is an adult with you,
you could hang the fans over a
candle flame. But be very careful
not to let the paper get anywhere
near the flame. And don't forget
to put out the candle afterwards.

Can you use a balloon to lift up a plastic beaker? Put the balloon inside the beaker and blow up the balloon. You will find that the sides of the balloon grip the beaker tightly. You should be able to lift up the beaker just by holding on to the neck of the balloon.

This works because air can be squeezed or compressed into a smaller space. The compressed air inside the balloon presses outwards on the sides of the beaker, so you can lift it up. Air pressure can be a powerful force.

The air around presses against us equally in all directions. The pressure of the air in any place is caused by the weight of all the air pressing down on that place. Things have weight because gravity pulls them to the ground. This test shows that air has weight.

Tie a piece of string to the middle of a thin stick and hang the string from a hook. Blow up two identical balloons, making one bigger than the other. Tie one balloon on to each end of the stick. The end with the bigger balloon will dip down. It is heavier than the smaller balloon because it contains more air.

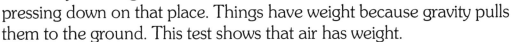

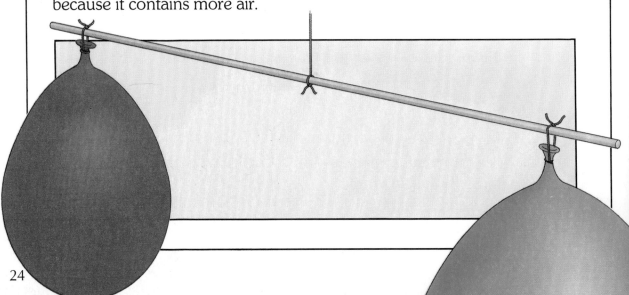

Upside-down Water

Hold a glass over a sink or a bowl and fill it right to the top with water. Carefully slide a smooth piece of card, such as a postcard, over the top. Hold your hand on the card and slowly turn the glass upside down. When you take away your hand, what happens?

What happens

The air pushes against the card and should keep the water in the glass. The pressure of the air upwards is greater than the pressure of the water downwards.

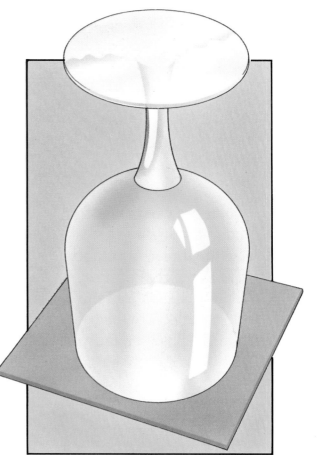

Make a Siphon

1. Fill two large jars with water. Hold some plastic tubing under water in a bowl until the air has escaped.
2. Pinch both tube ends and put one end under water in each jar. Lift one jar up and down.

What happens

When one jar is lower than the other, the air pressing down on the water in the top jar will force the water up the tube, and down into the other jar.

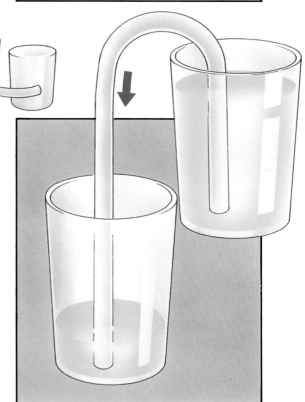

Make a Balloon Rocket

You will need:
a balloon, a straw, strong sticky tape, scissors, strong thread.

1. Cut a straw in half and push one end of a long piece of thread through the straw.
2. Tie the thread tightly across a room.
3. Cut two pieces of sticky tape.
4. Blow a little air into the balloon.
5. Hold the end of the balloon tightly so the air cannot escape and ask a friend to help you tape the balloon firmly to the straw.
6. Blow some more air into the balloon.

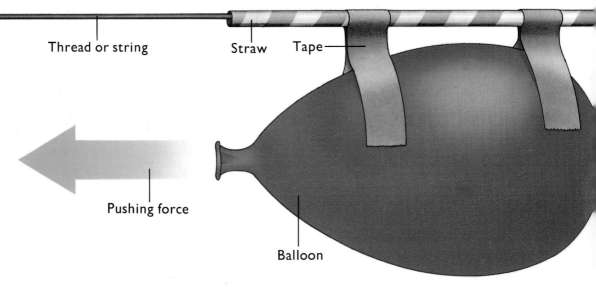

Thread or string   Straw   Tape

Pushing force

Balloon

7. When you let the balloon go, how fast does it travel? Can you think of a way of slowing down the rocket?
8. If you set up two balloon rockets side by side, you could have a race!

What happens
The air inside the balloon is squashed into a small space so it is at a high pressure. As it rushes out of the neck of the balloon, it pushes the balloon in the opposite direction. The hot gases rushing out of the back of a jet aeroplane push it forwards.

▲ Powerful fans on a hovercraft
blow air under the craft, which
increases the air pressure there.
This higher pressure pushes the
craft off the ground or water, so it
floats on a cushion of compressed
air. Propellers on the top of the
hovercraft spin round to push the
air aside and drive the hovercraft
backwards or forwards.

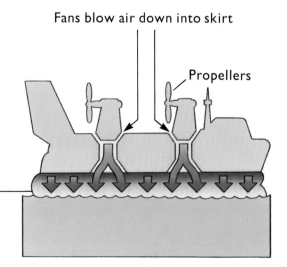

Fans blow air down into skirt

Propellers

Cushion of compressed air

WIND AND WEATHER

Weather is produced by air moving from place to place – which we call winds. Winds are caused by warm air rising and cooler air moving in to take its place. Warm air is lighter or less dense than cool air, so it creates low air pressure. Cool air is heavier or more dense and creates high air pressure. Usually we have fine weather when the air pressure is high. Low air pressure brings clouds, rain or snow.

▼ Winds can sometimes blow at tremendous speeds and cause great damage. The winds produced by a hurricane can travel at 120–160 kilometres an hour. This picture shows the damage from a hurricane in Darwin, Australia.

Make a Barometer

A barometer measures air pressure. A change in the air pressure tells us when the weather is likely to change.

You will need:
a tall, clear bottle, a saucer or dish, two thin pieces of wood, sticky tape, a pen.

1. Fill the bottle with water. Hold the saucer or dish over the top of the bottle and carefully turn the bottle upside down. Some of the water will spill out, so do this over a sink or a bowl.
2. Stand the saucer or dish with the bottle inside it in a cool place.
3. Tilt the bottle to let some air in. It needs to be about one-third full of air.
4. Slip the pieces of wood under the bottle to lift it clear of the saucer or dish. This lets water move in and out of the bottle.
5. Stick a long piece of tape on the side of the bottle and mark the level of the water.
6. Watch your barometer carefully and mark the level of the water at regular intervals. Can you predict the weather with your barometer?

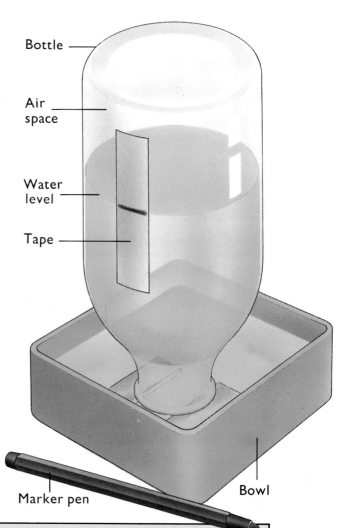

Bottle

Air space

Water level

Tape

Marker pen

Bowl

What happens
When the air pressure increases, it pushes down on the water in the dish, forcing the water up the bottle. When the air pressure falls, the level of water in the bottle falls too. Better weather will usually follow when the barometer rises and worse weather when it falls.

Make a Wind Sock

A wind sock at an airport shows the strength and direction of the wind and helps pilots to take off and land safely. Make a wind sock yourself.

1. Cut the shirt sleeve in half.
2. Ask an adult to help you bend the wire into a circle. Sew one end of the sleeve to the wire.
3. Tie a piece of string to one side of the circle.
4. Tie the string to a long pole, such as an old broom handle.
5. Put your wind sock outside.

You will need:
an old shirt sleeve or stocking, scissors, wire, string, a pole or long stick.

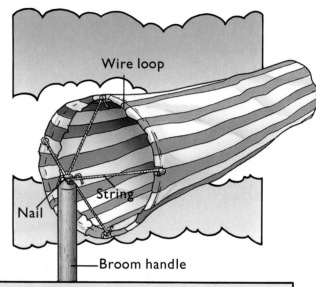

Wire loop

String

Nail

Broom handle

Measuring Wind Speed

You will need:
a cardboard box, dowel, a pen, cardboard, tape.

1. Cut off both ends of the box.
2. Draw a scale at one end.
3. Make a cardboard flap which will fit inside one end of the box.
4. Stick the flap to the dowel and push the dowel through the sides of the box. Make sure the flap of card can swing freely.
5. Stick an arrow on to the dowel and put the wind speed measurer outside facing into the wind. How much does the flap move?

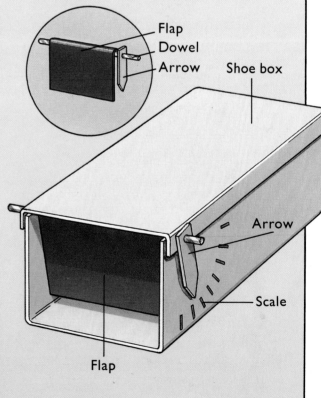

Flap
Dowel
Arrow
Shoe box

Arrow

Scale

Flap

Make a Windmill

You will need:
a long strip of 1 cm square wood, card, empty box, glue, sticky tape, 2 cotton reels, corrugated card, thin dowel, card or cloth, scissors, hacksaw.

1. Cut two short lengths of the one centimetre square wood and ask an adult to help you drill a hole through the centre point of each piece of wood.

2. Cut two small circles of card and make a hole in the middle of each circle.

3. Push a thin piece of dowel through the hole in one piece of card, through the hole in the one centimetre square wood and out through the other card circle. Glue the dowel to fix the wood in a cross shape.

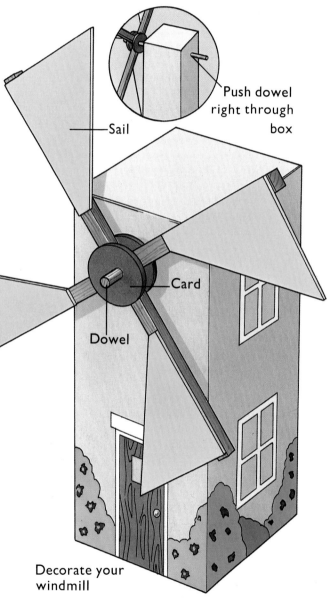

Push dowel right through box

Sail

Card

Dowel

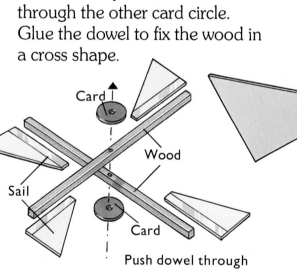

Card

Wood

Sail

Card

Push dowel through all holes and glue

4. Cut sails out of card or cloth and fix them to the wooden cross with glue or sticky tape.

5. Push the dowel through the top of the box.

Decorate your windmill

6. Put your windmill in a breeze outside or on a windowsill.

7. Can you use your windmill to lift something? Hint: fix a cotton reel to the dowel at the back of the box.

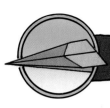

FLYING THINGS

How many flying things can you think of? Some flying things are alive. They are animals or parts of plants. Others are machines made by people.

You could make a scrapbook of flying things. Fill your scrapbook with drawings, postcards and pictures cut out of newspapers or magazines.

Can you make a piece of paper fly through the air? First, drop the paper from a height. As the sheet of paper falls, air is trapped underneath. As the air escapes, it makes the paper sway.

Fold the paper in half and open it out. Fold one of the long edges back. Drop the paper from a height again.

The centre fold makes the air pressure the same on both sides of the paper and this stops it rolling from side to side. Folding a long edge makes one side of the paper heavier, so the paper pushes through air more easily.

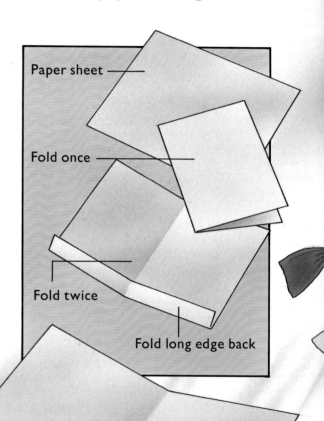

Paper sheet

Fold once

Fold twice

Fold long edge back

▲ Have you ever seen people hang gliding? As the wings of the glider move through the air, they help to lift the glider upwards. Warm air currents rising up from the ground also help to push the glider up into the sky.

Make a Frisbee

To find out more about how things move through the air, make a frisbee.

You will need:
thin balsa wood from a model shop (2–3 millimetres thick), elastic band, scissors, sandpaper, paints.

1. Use the scissors to cut two pieces of balsa wood about 2–3 centimetres wide by 12–20 centimetres long. The size of the pieces is not all that important so long as they are both the same size.
2. Rub the sandpaper over the wood to make it smooth on both sides.
3. Hold the two pieces of wood in a cross shape and wrap the elastic band round them to fix them in this position.
4. Paint your frisbee any colours you like.
5. Take your frisbee outside. Hold the tip of one piece of wood, lift the frisbee above your head and throw it into a breeze. Try to spin it as you

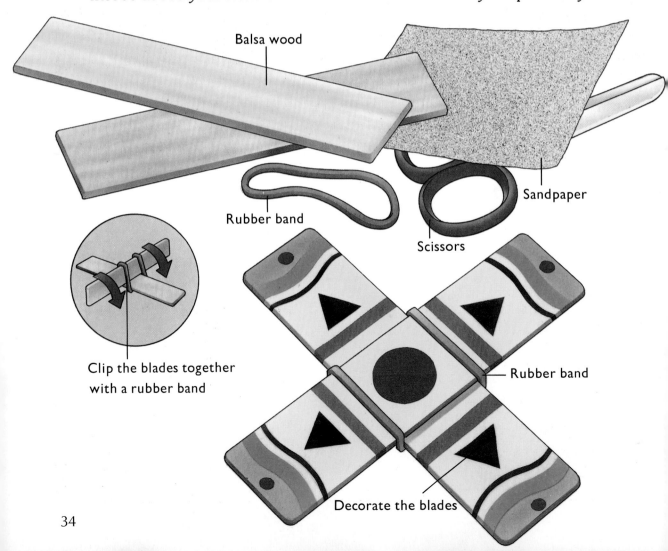

Balsa wood

Sandpaper

Rubber band

Scissors

Clip the blades together with a rubber band

Rubber band

Decorate the blades

throw. How far does it fly? If you round off the corners of the wood, does it fly further?

6. What happens if you fix the two pieces of wood so that one is standing up and the other lies flat?

▲ A gannet has a smooth, streamlined body shape, which helps it to fly fast through the air. You can find out more about birds and flight on pages 46–47.

What happens

As objects fly through the air, the air pulls against them and holds them back. This resistance to movement is called drag. Flying objects need enough energy to overcome drag and move through the air. By smoothing the wood with the sandpaper, you cut down the amount of drag. The frisbee with one piece of wood standing up creates a lot of air resistance and hardly flies at all. The flat frisbee creates less air resistance and flies much better.

Wings

Cut out a strip of paper about
20 centimetres long and
5 centimetres or more wide. Fold
the paper into a bridge shape and
put the bridge on a flat surface.
Blow steadily under the bridge.
What happens to the bridge?

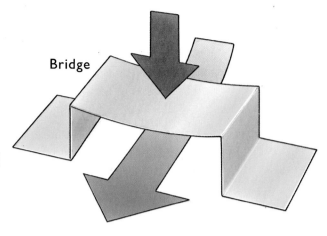

Bridge

Blow hard under the bridge

What happens

The top of the bridge moves down and the paper moves up. When air
moves fast, it is at a low pressure. Because the air pressure under the
bridge is low, the higher air pressure on top pushes the bridge down.
This link between air speed and air pressure is very important. It helps
all sorts of flying things, from swallows to aeroplanes, to fly.

Making Round Wings

1. Make a loop out of each strip
of paper. Overlap the ends and
tape them inside and outside the
loop to match the picture.
2. Push the straw through the
pockets in the loops.
3. How well does your straw
plane fly? Put the loops on the
top or the bottom of the straw
and in different positions along
the straw. How does this affect
the way the plane flies? Does the
plane fly better with the small or
the large loop in front?

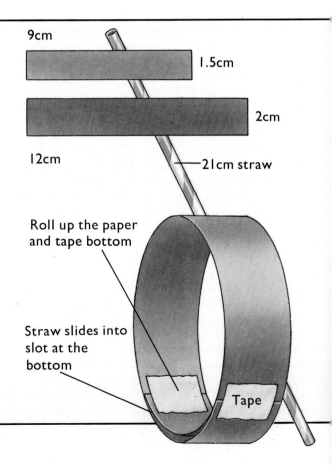

9cm

1.5cm

2cm

12cm

21cm straw

Roll up the paper
and tape bottom

Straw slides into
slot at the
bottom

Tape

Make a Wing

A wing is a special shape called an aerofoil.

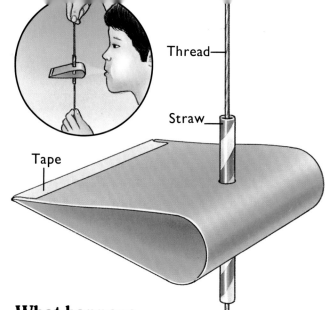

Thread

Straw

Tape

1. Cut a thin strip of paper about 4 cm wide and 26 cm long.
2. Cut a short length of straw.
3. Bend and fold the paper into a wing shape.
4. Use sticky tape to join the ends of the paper on top of the wing.
5. Push the straw through holes in the middle of the wing and fix it in place with tape.
6. Push a long piece of thread down through the straw.
7. Hold the thread and blow.

What happens

The air going over the top of the wing moves faster, and faster air means lower pressure. The slower air under the wing is at a higher pressure and pushes the wing up the thread. This upward pushing force is called lift.

What happens

The round wings on this plane work in the same way as flatter wings. The air moves more slowly under the wing and the higher air pressure lifts the plane up into the air.

Make Paper Gliders

Use A4-sized paper, about 30 centimetres by 20 centimetres. You can make paper gliders from different kinds of paper, such as newspaper, glossy magazine paper, crepe paper or tissue paper. What is the best kind of material for making paper gliders?

1. Fold the paper in half down the middle of the long side and open it out again.
2. Fold the top corners over so they meet in the middle.
3. Fold the same corners to the middle once more.
4. Turn the paper over.
5. Fold the sides to the middle and then fold the glider in half.
6. Grip the glider firmly by the centre fold and pull the wings flat.
7. Use sticky tape to hold the wings together in the middle.
8. Add one or more paper clips or a small piece of modelling clay to the nose of the glider. Does the glider fly better?
9. Cut some small flaps in the end of the wings. Bend the flaps up and down and see how this changes the direction the glider flies in (see pages 40–41).

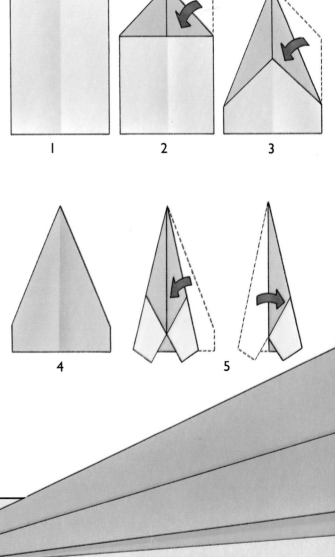

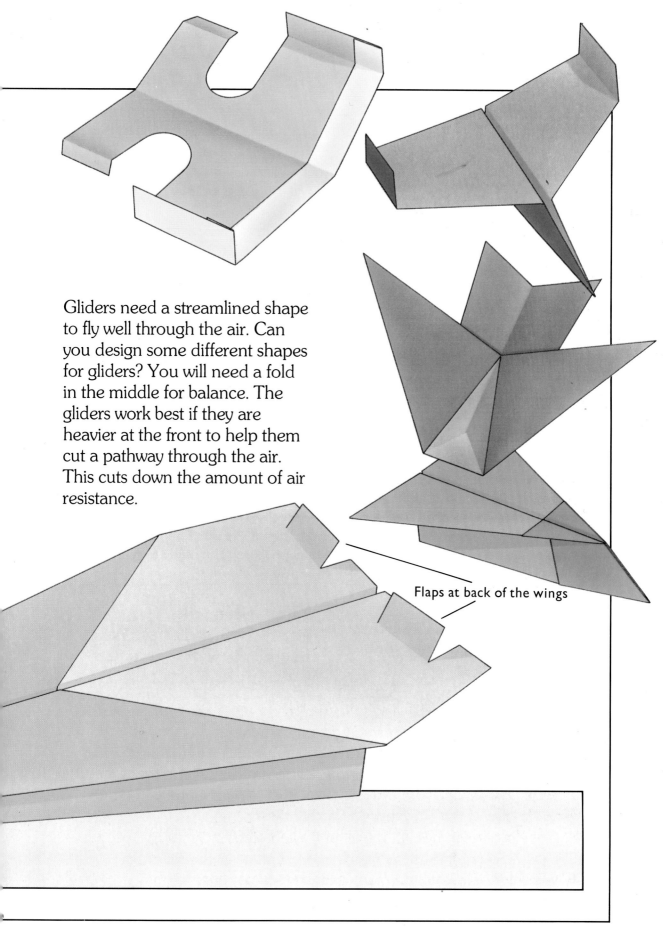

Gliders need a streamlined shape to fly well through the air. Can you design some different shapes for gliders? You will need a fold in the middle for balance. The gliders work best if they are heavier at the front to help them cut a pathway through the air. This cuts down the amount of air resistance.

Flaps at back of the wings

▲ To take off, a plane uses its engines to move fast along the runway. As it moves, air flows above and below the wings and produces lift. When there is enough lift to overcome the force of gravity, the plane takes off. In the air, the plane is slowed down by the resistance or drag of the air. The power of the engines has to overcome this dragging effect to keep the plane moving.

Making an Aeroplane

You will need:
a straw, paperclips, stiff paper, a pencil, sticky tape, scissors.

1. Make a wing shape, with the top edge curved, from a piece of stiff paper about 24 centimetres by 13 centimetres.
2. Tape the back edge of the wing and cut ailerons in this edge.
3. For the tail, cut a piece of stiff paper about 20 centimetres by 3.5 centimetres and fold the middle so it sticks up. Cut away about 1 centimetre of the flat pieces either side of the tail.
4. Cut elevators in the flat edges of the tail piece.
5. Use sticky tape to fix the wings and tail piece to the straw.
6. Weight the nose of the plane with several paperclips.

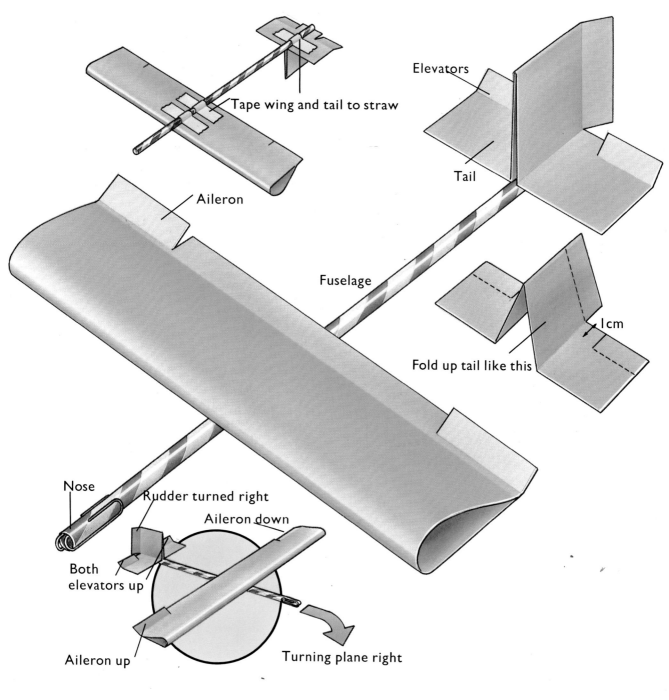

Tape wing and tail to straw

Elevators

Tail

Aileron

Fuselage

1cm

Fold up tail like this

Nose

Rudder turned right

Aileron down

Both elevators up

Aileron up

Turning plane right

7. Now bend the flaps up and down and the rudder from side to side to see how this affects the flight of the plane.

Have you ever noticed the flaps on the wings and tail piece of a passenger aeroplane? The flaps on the wings are called ailerons. The ones on the tail piece are called elevators. The pilot moves the ailerons and elevators, together with a tail flap called the rudder, to make the aeroplane turn, climb or dive through the air. Make your own aeroplane to see how this works.

Spinning Around

Have you *ever* watched a maple seed falling off a tree? As it spins round and round, the air rushing above and below the wing shape produces lift. This helps the seed to fly away from the parent tree. If it lands too near the parent, it is not likely to find enough space, light and water to grow into a new tree.

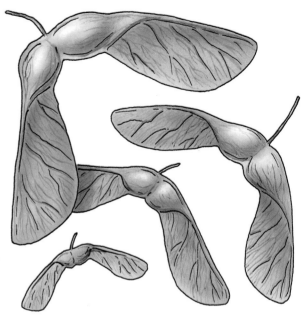

▼ Each one of the long, thin rotor blades on top of a helicopter is like the 'wing' of a maple seed. It is a long, narrow aerofoil. A helicopter stands still and turns its rotors to make air rush past its 'wings'. The faster the rotors spin, the faster the air moves and the more lift is produced.

Make a Paper Helicopter

1. On paper about
21 centimetres by 6 centimetres,
draw a shape like the picture.
2. Cut along the centre line.
3. Fold along the dotted line so
that one rotor bends forwards
and the other backwards.
4. Push a paperclip onto the
other end of the paper.
5. Drop your helicopter from a
height and watch how it spins.
6. Bend the rotors the other way.
In which direction does the
helicopter spin now?
7. Drop your helicopter upside-
down. Will it turn the right way up
again?

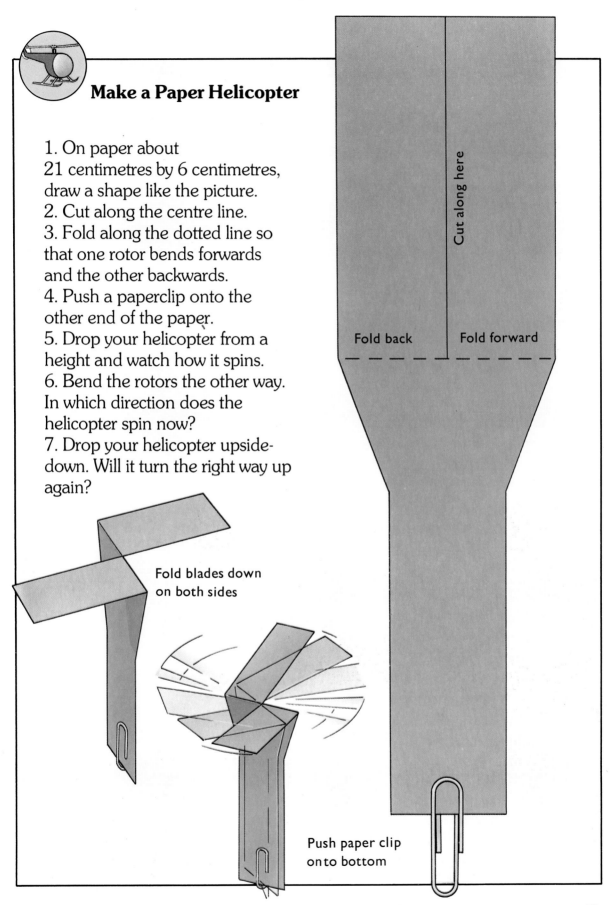

Cut along here

Fold back   Fold forward

Fold blades down
on both sides

Push paper clip
on to bottom

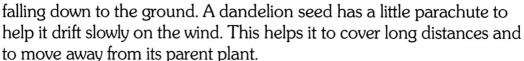

Drifting through the air

Air resistance can sometimes be useful if we want to slow flying things down. For instance, parachutes slow down things falling down to the ground. A dandelion seed has a little parachute to help it drift slowly on the wind. This helps it to cover long distances and to move away from its parent plant.

Make Parachutes

1. Cut some squares out of different materials. Make the squares different sizes.
2. Use tape to fix thread or string to each corner of the squares.
3. Tie a load to the strings under each parachute, and launch it.
4. How long does each parachute take to fall down to the ground? Do larger parachutes fall more quickly or more slowly? If the parachute is carrying a heavy load, does this make a difference?
5. Make a small hole in the top of one of the parachutes. How does this affect the way it falls down?

What happens
The force of gravity pulls the parachute down to the ground. But some air is trapped under the parachute. This air gets squashed, pushes up against the parachute and makes it fall more slowly.

▲ Modern parachutes have a hole in the top. This helps the air trapped inside the parachute to escape more smoothly and stops the parachute from wobbling and swaying as it falls through the air.

▶ Some animals, such as this colugo, have flaps of skin along the sides of the body. When they spread out this skin, they can glide through the air like living parachutes. The colugo can glide as far as 135 metres between trees.

FLYING ANIMALS

The first flying animals on Earth were probably insects. About 200 million years ago, winged reptiles called pterosaurs flew in the skies above the dinosaurs. The wings of pterosaurs were made of skin stretched between their arms and legs, rather like the wings of the bats alive today. The largest pterosaurs had wings that were as big as a small aeroplane.

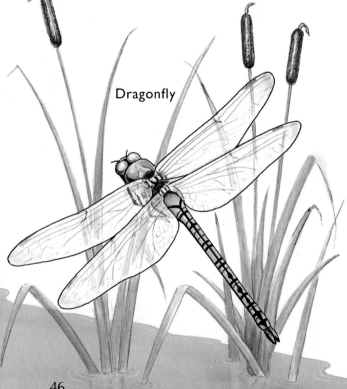

Dragonfly

Nowadays, only birds, bats and insects have wings to power flight upwards instead of just gliding along. Being able to fly is very useful. It helps animals to escape from danger as well as find food and places to nest.

Insects have very thin, flat wings with powerful muscles. As they flap their wings, they push against the air and this makes them move upwards and forwards. Flies can beat their wings as fast as 1000 times a second.

▲ As a bird's wings beat downwards, they create more air pressure under the wings. This extra pressure pushes the bird upwards. When the wings are pulled up again, the tips of the feathers move apart to let air flow through.

▼ Hummingbirds are like tiny helicopters. They can fly sideways, backwards and even upside-down. Hummingbirds beat their wings between 22 and 78 times a second and can fly up to 65 kilometres per hour.

Birds are well designed living flying machines. Their body is light in weight and some of their bones are hollow to reduce weight. Their feathers fit closely together to give them a smooth, streamlined shape. And their front arms have become wings. A bird's wing is shaped like an aerofoil to give it lift. Birds have very powerful chest muscles to beat their wings up and down.

TRUE OR FALSE?

1 Meringues are light because of all the air whisked into them.

2 Cold air is lighter or less dense than warm air.

3 Air cannot be squashed into a small space.

6 Bats have feathers on their wings.

4 Low air pressure usually brings bad weather.

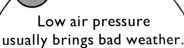

5 Flaps on the wings and tail of aeroplanes help them to climb, turn and dive.

Answers

1 True. All the bubbles of air make meringues light and fluffy.

2 False. Cold air is heavier or more dense than warm air, which will rise.

3 False. Air can be squashed or compressed into small spaces. Bicycle tyres are pumped full of compressed air.

4 True. With low air pressure, air rises and cools to form clouds.

5 True. The flaps control the way air flows over the wings. They allow the pilot to change the position of the aircraft.

6 False. The wings of a bat are made of skin. Only

Colour and Light

Can monkeys see in colour? Which colours stand out best from a distance? What are the primary colours of paint? How can you make coloured dyes from plants? Which kitchen chemicals are acids or alkalis? Which colours make up a television picture? How many colours are there in a rainbow? How do colour filters work? Why is the sky blue?

This section will help you to discover the answers to these questions and has lots of ideas for ways to investigate colour and light.

COLOUR AND LIGHT

In this section, you can discover how we see colours, how we use colours for painting and printing and how light is made up of all the colours of the rainbow.

The section is divided into eight different topics. Look out for the big headings with a circle at each end – like the one at the top of this page.

Pages 52–53

How Many Colours?

Collecting and sorting colours.

Pages 58–61

Painting Colours

Mixing colours; brushes and textures.

Pages 54–57

Seeing Colours

Animal eyes; colour blindness; safety colours.

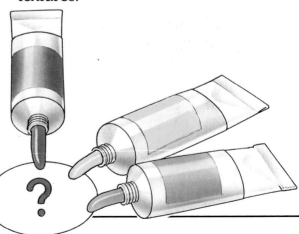

Making Colours

Pages 62–71

Colouring materials; natural pigments; dyeing cloth; acids and alkalis; chromatography; colours in books and on television.

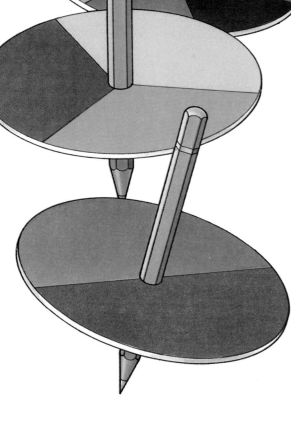

Rainbow Colours

Pages 72–75

Rainbow colours in water, oil, soap bubbles and some shells.

See-through Colours

Pages 76–79

Transparent materials; colour filters.

Coloured Light

Pages 80–85

Mixing light; sky colours; colours in space.

Animal Colours

Pages 86–87

Warning colours; camouflage colours; attracting a mate.

HOW MANY COLOURS?

Make a collection of different coloured objects like the ones along the *edges* of these two pages. Look for some natural materials as well as artificial ones. Sort your collection into sets such as happy and sad colours or summer and winter colours. How many different shades of the same colour can you find?

Another way of sorting your collection would be to put all the things made from the same material (such as paper, plastic or cloth) together.

▶ How many different colours can you find in the picture? What is your favourite colour?

SEEING COLOUR

We see things because light bounces off objects into our eyes. This 'bouncing off' effect is called reflection. The light from the Sun or an electric light bulb looks white, but it is really made up of all the colours of the rainbow. (see pages 72–75). The colours we see depend on the colours that are reflected off objects into our eyes. For instance, a tomato looks red because it reflects red light and absorbs the other colours.

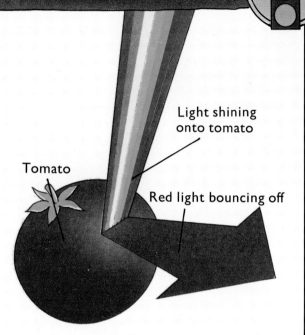

Light shining onto tomato

Tomato

Red light bouncing off

If an object absorbs all the rainbow colours in light, no light is reflected and we see black. If an object reflects all the colours, we see white.

Animal Eyesight

Did you know that many animals, such as cats, dogs, horses and cows, cannot see the colours we see? Their world is full of shades of black and white and grey. Apes and monkeys, however, seem to be able to see the same colours that we can and some animals, especially birds, may have better colour vision than we do. Animals that are brightly coloured can nearly always see colours.

Your view

Dog's view

Eye Colours

We see colours because of special cells that make up part of the lining of the eyeball. These cells are cone-shaped, so they are called cones. In each eye, there are about 7 million cones. One type of cone responds to red light, a second type responds to green light and a third type responds to blue light. The cones send messages to the brain and, by joining together the messages it receives, the brain tells us what colours we are seeing.

This test shows you more about how you see colours. Draw a red shape on a piece of white paper. Stare hard at your drawing for a minute. Then stare at a blank piece of white paper. What colour is your drawing now? Repeat the test with a blue object.

What happens

The cones that respond to red light quickly get tired so they stop working for a while. When you stare at the white paper, only the green and blue cones are working. So you see a greeny-blue picture. This colour is called cyan. With the blue object, only the red and green cones are working, so you see yellow.

Colour Blindness

Some people are colour blind, which means they cannot tell the difference between certain colours. Very few people are truly colour blind and see only black, white and grey.

 **Colour Messages**

Which colours stand out best from a distance? Stick paper of one colour on to different backgrounds, or different colours on to the same background.

     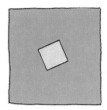 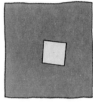

Same background   Different background

Ask a friend to hold up each mixture of colours at a distance. Which combination of two colours stands out best? Are some colours more affected by the background colour than others? Decide which colours you would use for signs in a desert, a snowy mountain or a forest.

 Remembering Colours

Are some colours easier to remember than others? Look at this picture for a minute. Then shut the book. How many of the objects can you remember? Can you remember the colour of each object? You could record your results and compare them with those of your friends.

Safety Colours

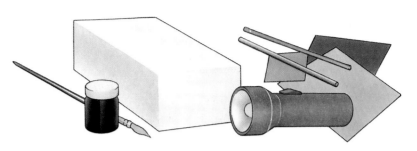

At night or in a dark room, it is hard to see the colour of anything. This is because the cones in your eyes need a lot of light to work properly. But some colours have to stand out at night, in the dim light of tunnels or cinemas or be clearly seen by people with poor eyesight. Which colours show up well in dim light?

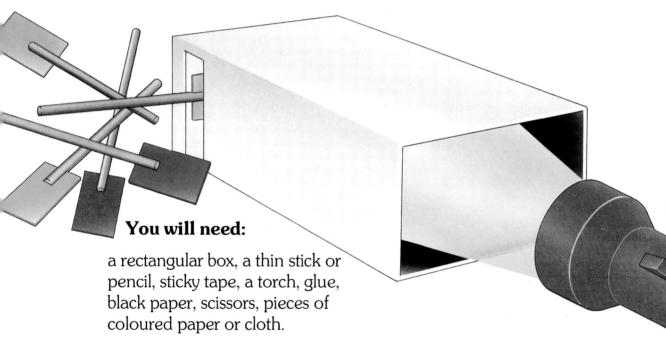

You will need:

a rectangular box, a thin stick or pencil, sticky tape, a torch, glue, black paper, scissors, pieces of coloured paper or cloth.

1. Cut off one end of the box and cut a slit in one side of the box near the other end.
2. Cover the inside of the box with black paper.
3. Cut small pieces of the paper or cloth.
4. Stick each piece of paper or cloth in turn on to the stick or pencil and poke it through the slit in the box.
5. Shine a torch into the open end of the box. Which colours show up best in the dim light?

PAINTING COLOURS

Paints used to be made from natural pigments, which are coloured powders formed by grinding up materials such as soil, rocks, plants, shellfish or even dead insects. All these things have a natural colour. Nowadays, chemists use both natural and artificial pigments to produce paints.

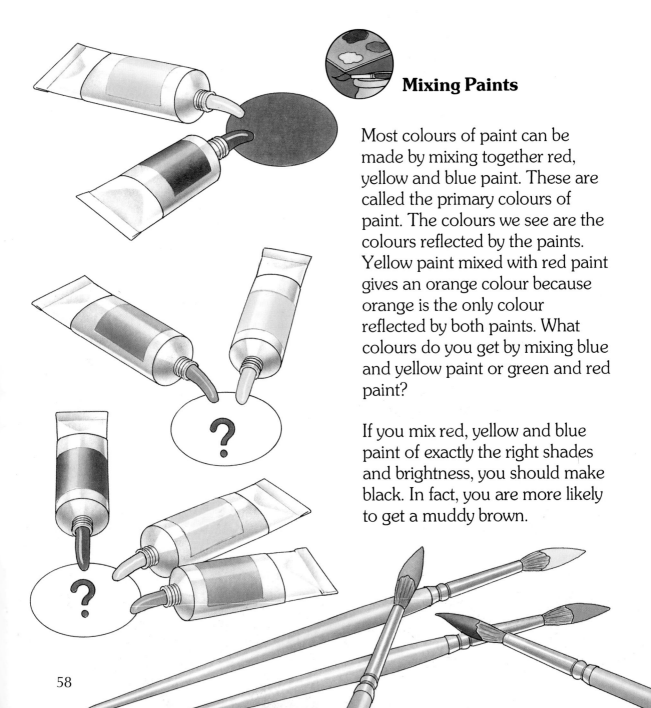

Mixing Paints

Most colours of paint can be made by mixing together red, yellow and blue paint. These are called the primary colours of paint. The colours we see are the colours reflected by the paints. Yellow paint mixed with red paint gives an orange colour because orange is the only colour reflected by both paints. What colours do you get by mixing blue and yellow paint or green and red paint?

If you mix red, yellow and blue paint of exactly the right shades and brightness, you should make black. In fact, you are more likely to get a muddy brown.

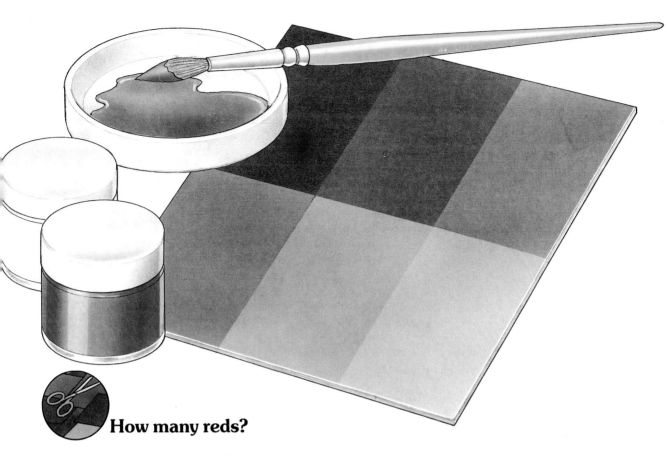

How many reds?

Have you ever looked at the paint charts in do-it-yourself stores? You can buy lots of different shades of one colour and it is often hard to choose the right one for your room.

See if you can mix up six shades of one colour, such as red. Divide up a piece of paper into six equal sized strips. Put bright red in the first strip and then keep adding white paint, a little at a time, to make lighter reds. When the paint is dry, write a number on the back of each strip. Make one the deepest colour and six the palest colour. Then cut up all the squares and mix them up. Can you sort them back into the right order?

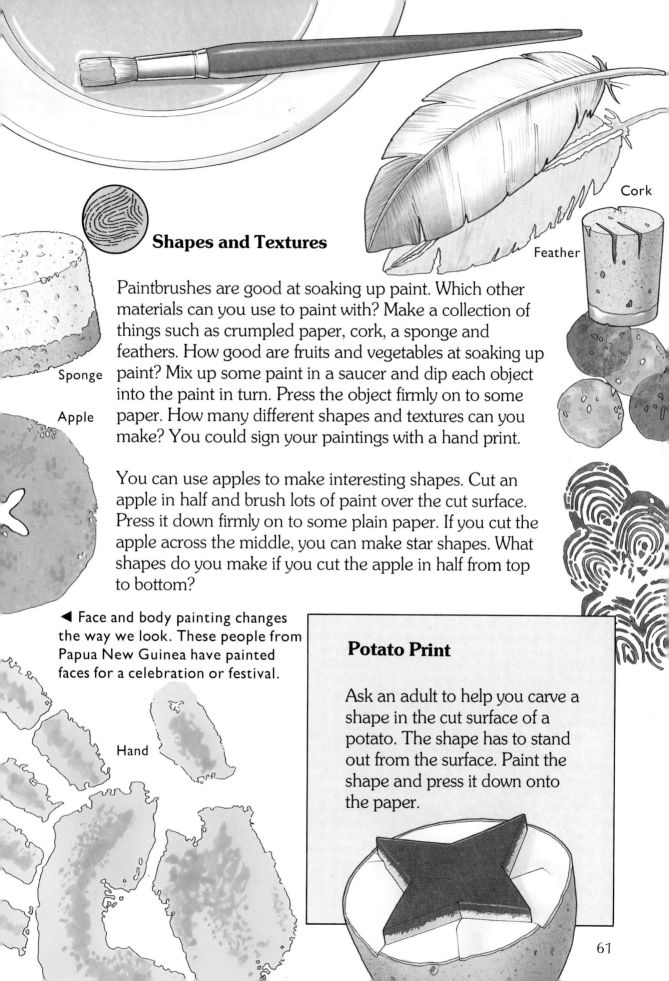

Shapes and Textures

Paintbrushes are good at soaking up paint. Which other materials can you use to paint with? Make a collection of things such as crumpled paper, cork, a sponge and feathers. How good are fruits and vegetables at soaking up paint? Mix up some paint in a saucer and dip each object into the paint in turn. Press the object firmly on to some paper. How many different shapes and textures can you make? You could sign your paintings with a hand print.

Sponge

Apple

You can use apples to make interesting shapes. Cut an apple in half and brush lots of paint over the cut surface. Press it down firmly on to some plain paper. If you cut the apple across the middle, you can make star shapes. What shapes do you make if you cut the apple in half from top to bottom?

◄ Face and body painting changes the way we look. These people from Papua New Guinea have painted faces for a celebration or festival.

Hand

Cork

Feather

Potato Print

Ask an adult to help you carve a shape in the cut surface of a potato. The shape has to stand out from the surface. Paint the shape and press it down onto the paper.

MAKING COLOURS

As well as paints, there are several other colouring materials, such as wax crayons, colouring pencils, chalk, charcoal, ink and felt pens. Draw an outline shape several times and colour each one in with a different colouring material. How do they look different? Which colouring material is easiest to use? Which do you like best? What happens if you put the colouring materials on a wet surface? Do they mix with water?

▼ Stone Age artists painted the walls of these caves between 12,000 and 30,000 years ago. They mixed up their colours from natural pigments in the soil, rocks or minerals. They ground up these pigments into a smooth paste with simple tools called pestles and mortars, and mixed the colours together on the stones. They probably added some animal fat to make the colours waterproof. The artists used brushes made of animal hair, chewed twigs and pads of moss and fur. All their paintings were done using only the flickering light from small lamps which burnt animal fat.

Making yellow dye

You will need:
60 grams of alum, 1 tablespoon of cream of tartar, 30 grams of onion skins, cloth, a sieve, 2 large saucepans, a jar.

You can use the coloured juices from plants to dye cloth or wool. Some dyes do not give permanent colours unless another chemical is added. These chemicals are called mordants. They 'fix' the colour by making it bite into the cloth so the colours last. In the past, tree bark and wood ash have been used as mordants. Nowadays, you can buy artificial mordants from the chemist.

Cream of Tartar

Alum

1. Mix the alum and cream of tartar with 500 millilitres of warm water in the jar. Add to a large pan of cold water.
2. Put the cloth in the pan and ask an adult to help you heat it gradually. Stir until it boils.
3. Simmer gently for about an hour, then leave to cool down.
4. Take out the cloth and leave it in a plastic bag.
5. Ask an adult to help you boil the onion skins in a deep pan full of water and simmer for an hour.
6. Strain the liquid through a sieve to get rid of the skins.
7. Put your damp cloth into the pan and boil up the water again. Simmer gently for one hour.
8. Switch off the heat and leave the pan to cool.
9. Take the cloth out of the pan and rinse it thoroughly.
10. Leave the cloth to dry.

Other colours from plants

Now make dyes from other plants, such as spinach, tea leaves, red cabbage, pine cones and blackberries. You can also dye wool instead of cloth.

Coloured Patterns

There are several different ways of making coloured patterns in cloth. In tie-dyeing, part of the cloth is tied up to stop the dye from reaching that part of the cloth. When the tie is removed, white patterns are left in the coloured material. If you do this yourself, you can knot the cloth or use string or sew stitches to tie the cloth. You could also try tying different 'ties' or putting objects such as pebbles, buttons and seeds in the cloth to create a different pattern.

You can also make different colours by dyeing the same piece of material in several colours, one after another.

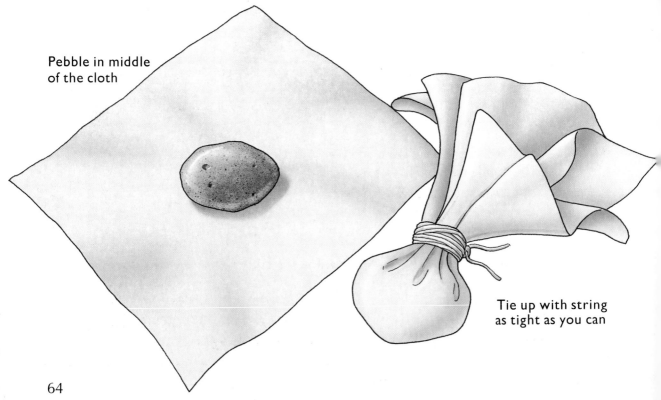

Pebble in middle of the cloth

Tie up with string as tight as you can

▲ Cloth that has been tie-dyed can be used to make all sorts of clothing.

◀ Batik dyeing involves dropping hot, melted wax on to the cloth. The waxed areas do not take up the dye and when the wax is washed off, it leaves beautiful patterns in the cloth. You can see how this works by drawing a picture with a wax crayon or an unlit candle and then painting over it.

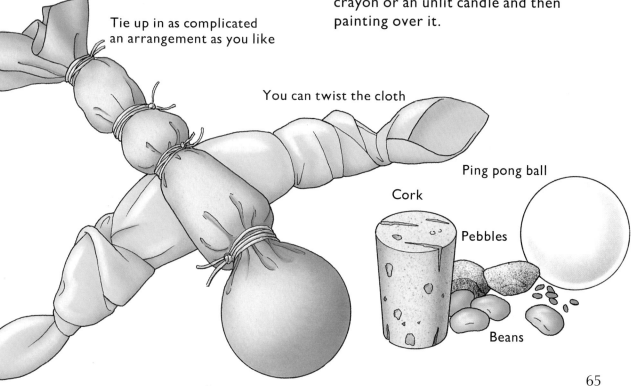

Tie up in as complicated an arrangement as you like

You can twist the cloth

Ping pong ball

Cork

Pebbles

Beans

Kitchen Chemicals

You can use a solution of coloured dye to find out if the chemicals in the kitchen are acids or alkalis. Acids and alkalis are chemical opposites. They behave differently when they are mixed with other chemicals. A dye that changes colour when it is mixed with acids or alkalis is called an indicator. You can make an indicator from red cabbage.

1. Chop up some red cabbage leaves and put them in a bowl.
2. Add a little sand and mash up the leaves with the back of an old spoon. The sand helps to break up the cabbage leaves so the dye can get out.
3. Ask an adult to add some very hot water to the bowl. Leave the cabbage to soak until cool.
4. Pour the liquid through a sieve

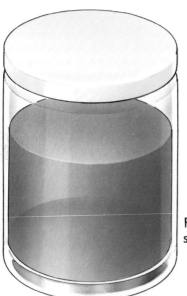

Put dye in screw top jar

to get rid of the cabbage leaves. You will be left with a coloured indicator solution. Put this into a bottle or jar with a lid.
5. In a saucer or a jar, mix a small amount of the indicator solution with some of the different chemicals in the kitchen. Good things to try are lemon juice, baking powder, vinegar, washing powder and soapy water.

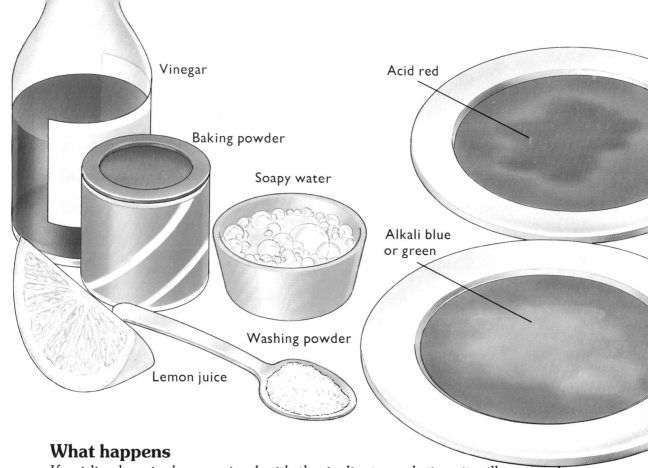

Vinegar

Baking powder

Soapy water

Acid red

Alkali blue or green

Washing powder

Lemon juice

What happens

If acidic chemicals are mixed with the indicator solution, it will turn red or orange. If the chemicals are alkaline, the solution will turn blue or green. How many acids and alkalis can you find?

Did You Know?

The poison in a bee sting is an acid and the poison in a wasp sting is an alkali.

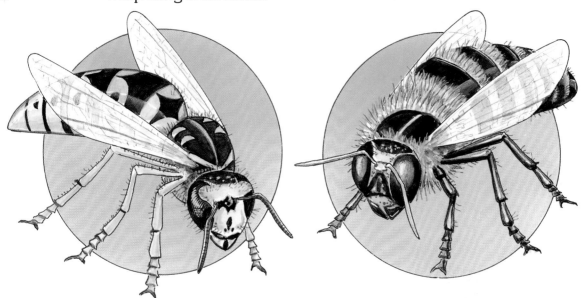

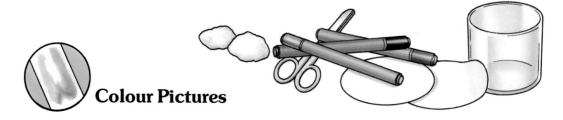

Colour Pictures

Many of the pigments we use appear to be one colour but are really made up of mixtures of colours. You can separate out these colours using a technique called chromatography – the word means 'colour pictures'.

You will need:
felt-tip pens (especially dark colours such as brown and black), a pencil, sticky tape, a beaker of water, blotting paper, scissors, cotton wool.

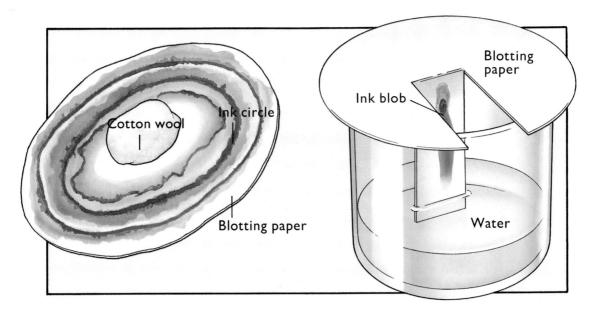

1. Cut up several small circles of blotting paper.
2. Put a ring of colour in the middle of the circles.
3. Soak a ball of cotton wool in some water and put it in the middle of the coloured rings. Watch the colours spread out.
4. Cut a strip in some of the circles to match the picture.
5. Put a small dot of colour on the bottom of the strip.
6. Put some water in the beaker and let the strip hang down so it just touches the water. Before you put each strip in the water, see if you can guess which colours you will see.
7. Now try other sources, such as food colouring, inks and sweets.

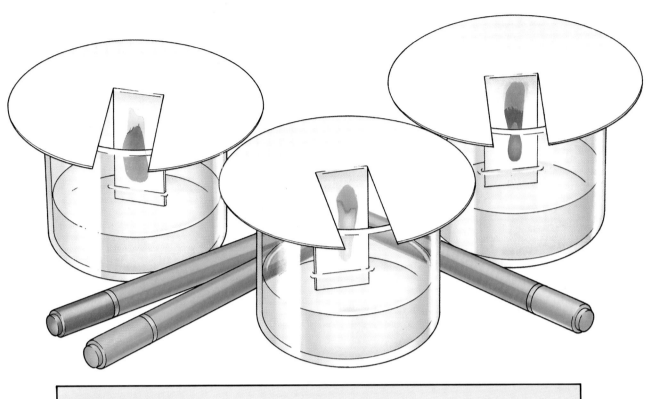

What happens

As the water spreads through the blotting paper, it carries the colour with it. If the pens are made up of several different pigments, you will see bands of different colours. Some pigments contain bigger, heavier particles than others so the pigments spread out at different speeds. Smaller, lighter particles move faster and further, leaving the bigger ones behind.

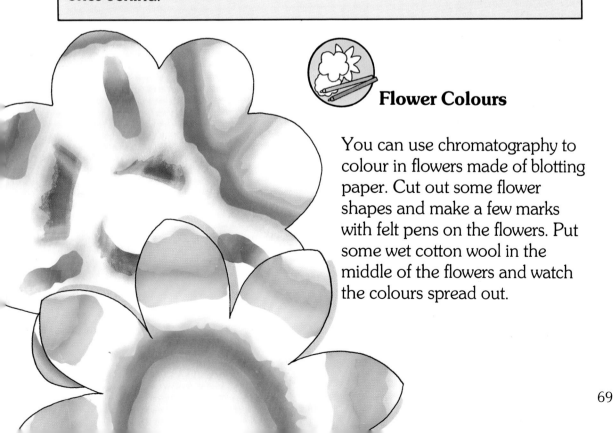

Flower Colours

You can use chromatography to colour in flowers made of blotting paper. Cut out some flower shapes and make a few marks with felt pens on the flowers. Put some wet cotton wool in the middle of the flowers and watch the colours spread out.

Lots of Dots

Use a magnifying glass to look closely at the pictures in a newspaper. You will see that each one is made up of lots of black dots. The dots are largest in the dark areas and very small in the pale areas. The pale areas look grey, even though only black ink is used.

Book Colours

The colour pictures in a book are also made up of lots of dots. The original picture is broken down into four colours – the primary pigments red, blue and yellow, plus black. The black helps to add in fine detail and make some areas darker.

Each colour is printed as tiny dots. Because the dots are so small, our eyes can't see them – unless we use a magnifying glass. So we see areas of flat colour, which look like the original colours of the picture. If the dots are not printed in exactly the right place, the picture looks fuzzy.

Blue is a blue-green colour called cyan

Red is a pinky colour called

Dotty television

The colours of a television picture are also made up of a pattern of tiny coloured dots of light. From a distance, these dots merge together to make a many-coloured picture and we are not aware of the dots. A television picture is made up of red, blue and green dots because these are the primary colours of light. They are different from the primary colours of paint (see page 58).

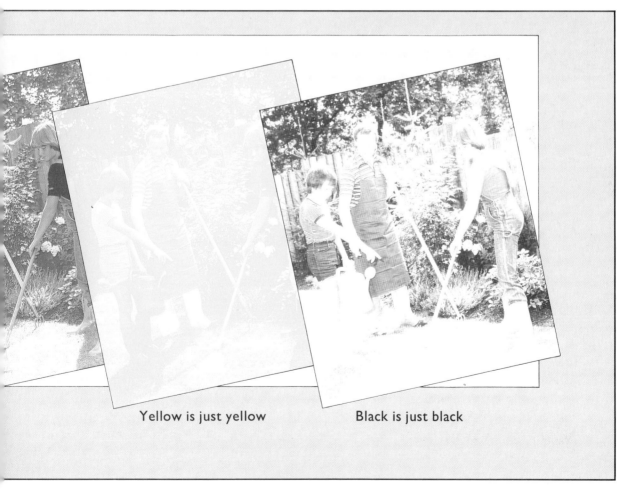

Yellow is just yellow   Black is just black

▲ Have you ever seen a rainbow on a sunny day when it is raining? Rainbows sometimes appear in the spray of water from a waterfall too. The raindrops or water drops make the light spread out so we can see the different colours. Some people think they can see the seven different colours in a rainbow – red, orange, yellow, green, blue, indigo and violet. How many colours can you see in a rainbow?

RAINBOW COLOURS

Where have you seen rainbow colours? Take a bowl of water out into some bright sunshine. Put a few drops of oil on the surface of the water. How many colours can you see? What happens if you add more water or more oil? If you stir the water with a stick, do the colours change?

Soap bubbles also have rainbow colours in them. Do big bubbles have different colour patterns from small bubbles? Do the colours in a bubble change in sunlight?

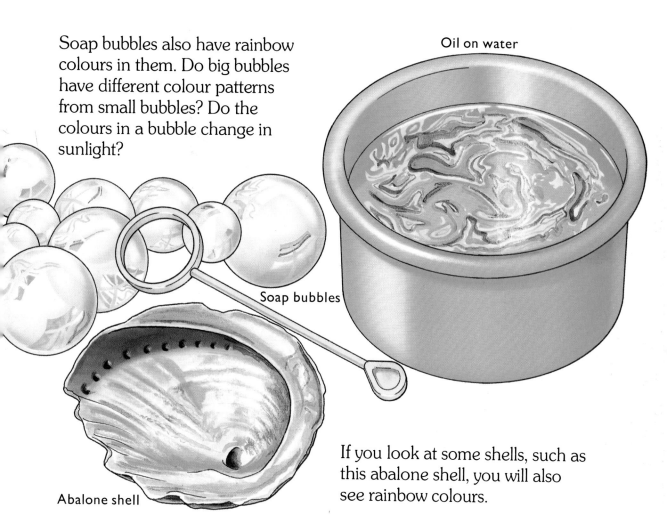

Oil on water

Soap bubbles

Abalone shell

If you look at some shells, such as this abalone shell, you will also see rainbow colours.

The colours in oil, soap bubbles and some shells are caused by the way light is reflected between the thin outer layers of each object. The rainbow colours are not spread out as they are in a real rainbow.

A Prism Rainbow

A specially shaped piece of glass called a prism will spread out the colours in white light to make rainbow colours. This was first seen by the famous scientist Isaac Newton, when carrying out some experiments in 1665.

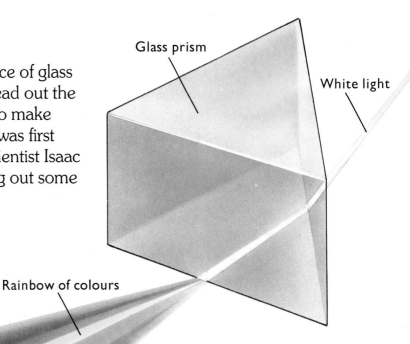

Glass prism

White light

Rainbow of colours

Make a Rainbow

You can make your own prism with a shallow dish of water and a mirror. Fill the dish with water and hold the mirror at an angle so that sunlight or electric light falls on the mirror. The water in front of the mirror works like a prism, making the light bend. The different colours in the light bend different amounts so the colours separate out. The mirror reflects the rainbow on to a wall or ceiling.

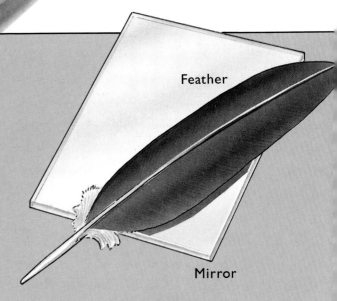

Feather

Mirror

Feather Rainbow

Ask an adult to light a candle for you. Stand about 30 centimetres away from the candle and look through the feather's outer edge. You see tiny flames with rainbow colours, because you look through narrow slits.

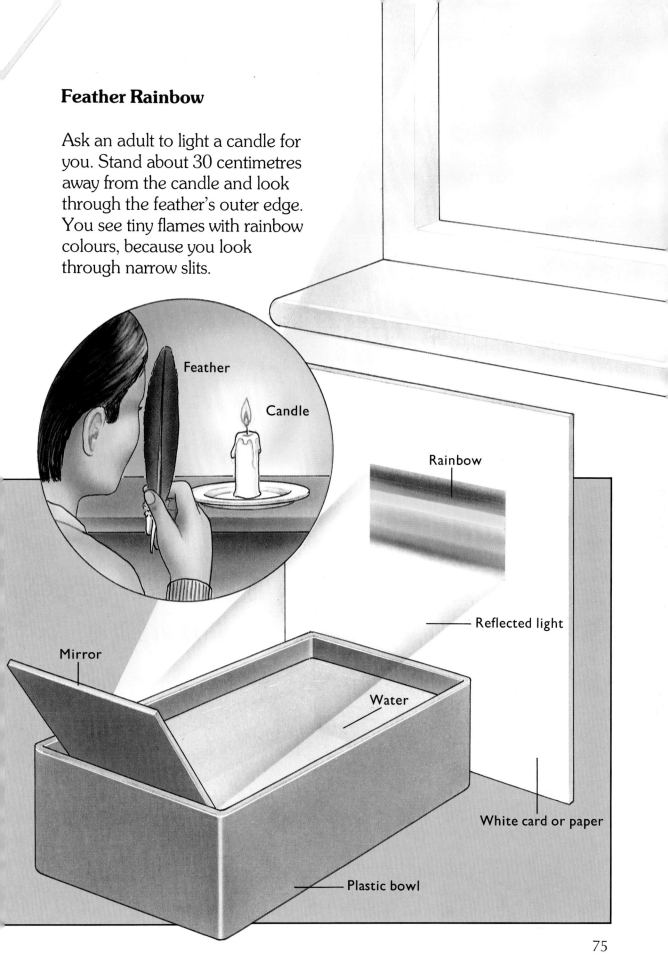

Feather

Candle

Rainbow

Reflected light

Mirror

Water

White card or paper

Plastic bowl

SEE-THROUGH COLOURS

Some materials, such as clear glass, perspex and water will let light pass through them. They are said to be transparent. If you look through transparent materials, they change the colours of the things you see.

Make a collection of transparent materials, such as coloured bottles, sweet wrappings and plastic. You could also colour the water in a clear bottle with ink or food colouring. How do these materials change the colour of things you see through them? Is there any difference if you overlap two colours?

What happens

The transparent materials are all types of filter. They let light of the same colour pass through but they stop other colours getting through. For instance, a red filter lets red light through, but stops the other colours.

▲ If you look at the light coming through a stained glass window, it will be the same colours as the glass itself. Each piece of glass only lets through light of the same colour as itself.

Strong light

Hole in top

Coloured film

Front slot

Make a Colour Box

You will need:
a large cardboard box with a lid, scissors, sticky tape, pieces of transparent coloured material (such as acetate), objects to put inside the box, a torch.

1. Collect some small objects which should include all the colours of the rainbow.
2. Cut a large square hole in the lid of the box.
3. Cut a thin, narrow hole in one side of the box.
4. Cut a square of each colour of transparent material. Make each square a little bit bigger than the hole in the top of the box.
5. Put the objects in the box.
6. Lay one of the pieces of transparent material over the hole in the top of the box and ask a friend to shine a light down through the transparent material.
7. When you look through the hole in the side of the box, what colour do the objects appear to be? Repeat the same test with the other transparent materials and record your results. Can you explain your results? (Hint: look back at filters on page 76.)

Make Some Colour Glasses

You will need:

stiff card, scissors, sticky tape, small pieces of red and green cellophane, pencils.

1. Cut out the glasses from the cardboard.
2. Stick red cellophane over one eye piece and green cellophane over the other eye piece.
3. Put on the glasses and see how they change colours around you.

What happens

The red eye piece lets only red light reach your eye and the green eye piece lets only green light reach your eye. So one eye sees only things that reflect red light and the other eye sees only things that reflect green light.

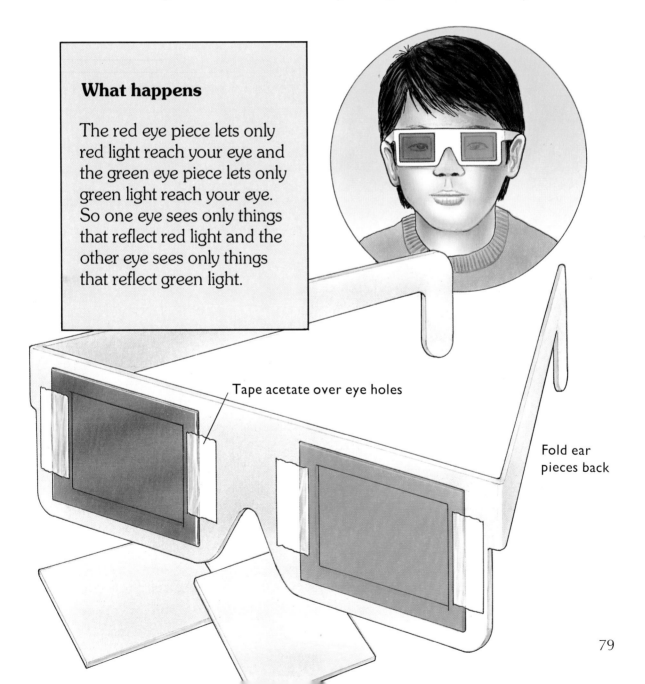

Tape acetate over eye holes

Fold ear pieces back

COLOURED LIGHT

Mixing coloured light does not give the same results as mixing coloured paints. This investigation shows how it is different.

You will need:
three torches, pieces of red, blue and green cellophane, sticky tape, white card.

1. Cut pieces of cellophane which are the right size to fit over the front of the torches. Make one torch red, one torch blue and one torch green.
2. In a darkened room, shine the red and green torches on to the white card. Where the beams of light meet on the card, you should see yellow light.
3. Try mixing blue and green light or blue and red light. What colours do they make?
4. Now try mixing all three colours. What happens this time?

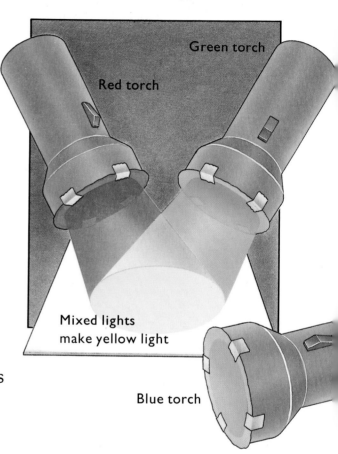

Green torch

Red torch

Mixed lights make yellow light

Blue torch

What happens
All the colours of the rainbow can be made by mixing the primary colours of light, which are red, blue and green. Can you remember the primary colours of paint? The colours you make by mixing the primary colours of either light or paint are called secondary colours. Yellow is one secondary colour of light. The others are dark pink (magenta) and green-blue (cyan). By mixing all three primary colours of light, you make white light.

▲ Coloured lights are often mixed together in different ways to change the atmosphere and create special effects at concerts. Colour filters are put in front of white spotlights to light up the stage and make the different colours.

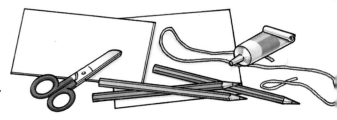

Make a Colour Changer

1. Cut out a cardboard circle about 10 centimetres across.
2. Cut out a circle from the white paper the same size as the card.
3. Colour in the paper circle with the same colours as the picture.
4. Glue the paper circle on to the cardboard.
5. Use a sharp pencil to make a hole in the middle of the circle.
6. Cut off about a metre of the string or wool.
7. Push the string or wool through the holes and knot the ends.
8. To spin your colour changer, move the circle to the middle of the string. Twirl it around several times to twist the wool or string. Then pull the string or wool very tight so the circle unwinds. As it unwinds, relax the wool or string and the circle will wind itself up again.

What happens

The colour changer makes the colours go by so fast that your eye can't see each one separately. Your brain combines some of the colours to make new ones. For instance, your brain turns flashes of blue and red into purple.

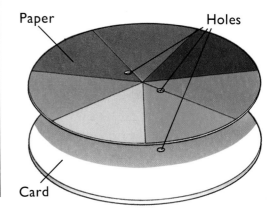

Paper   Holes

Card

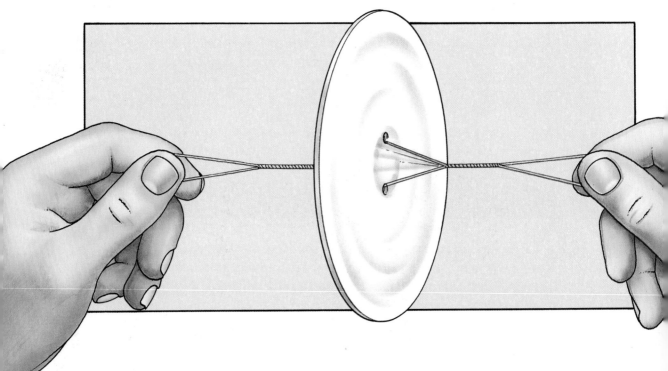

Spinning Colours

Another way to make coloured light mix by movement is to make some spinning tops. Cut some cardboard circles and colour each one in a different mixture of colours. Put a sharp pencil through the middle of each circle and twirl the pencil to make the tops spin. What happens to the colours?

If you make a spinning top with all the colours of the rainbow, it will look white or yellowish when you spin it. All the rainbow colours combine to make white light again.

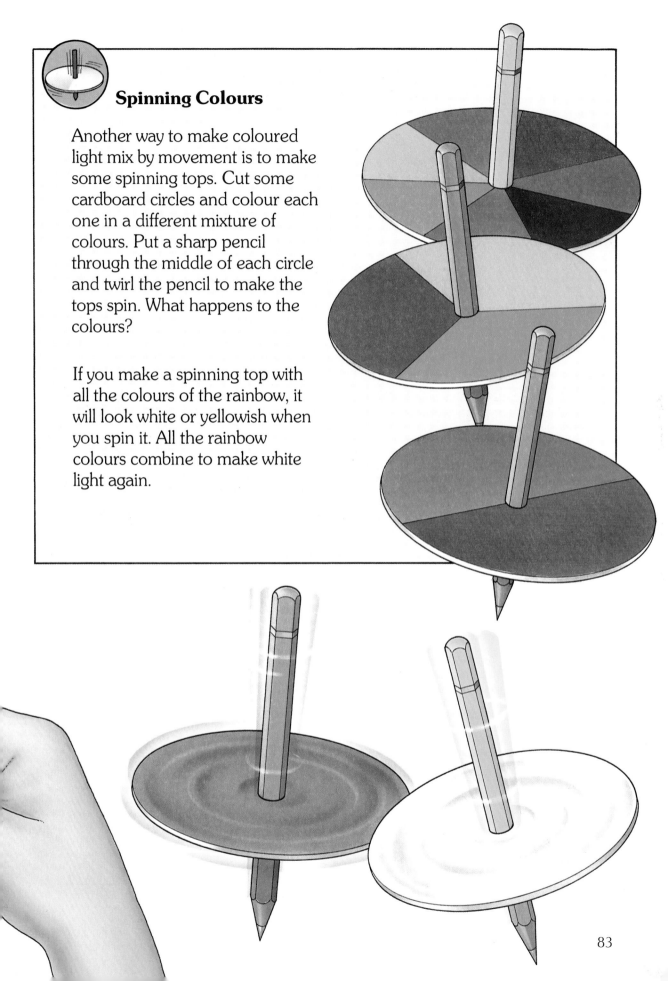

Sky Colours

Have you ever wondered why the sky often appears blue by day and red, pink or orange at sunrise or sunset? This investigation will show you why this happens.

Fill a tall, clear container with water and put about half a teaspoon of coffee whitener into the water. Don't stir the water. If you shine a torch on to the water from above, it will look a bluish-grey colour. Now shine a torch through the container from behind. You will find that the water looks an orange-pink colour. Try keeping a record of sky colours. What changes occur during a day or a week?

What happens

The Earth is wrapped in a blanket of invisible gases called the atmosphere. The atmosphere contains billions and billions of particles that are too small to see. When sunlight hits these particles, the light bounces off them and scatters. Blue and violet light scatter the most, orange and red light scatter the least.

When the Sun is low in the sky, at sunrise and sunset, its rays travel through a thicker layer of atmosphere than at midday. Most of the blue is scattered out of the light and only red and orange light is left to colour the sky. The same thing happens when you hold the torch behind the glass. At midday, the Sun is high in the sky so less light is scattered and more blue light reaches your eyes. This is why the liquid looks blue when you hold the torch above the glass.

Volcano Colours

After a volcanic eruption on Earth, there are lots of fine particles floating in the atmosphere. Winds carry these particles around the world. The dust particles scatter aside the blue light allowing only orange-red light to reach the Earth. That is why there are often spectacular sunsets after a big volcanic eruption.

▼ The planet Jupiter is made up mostly of whirling clouds of hydrogen. Other substances are mixed in with the hydrogen and form dark or coloured bands. Close-up photographs show red, green and blue colours in these clouds, which are always changing. The Great Red Spot on Jupiter is a gigantic cloud, which is larger than the Earth.

The colours of animals help them to survive in many different ways. They may help them to hide or to attract a mate. Some animals can even change colour if their surroundings change.

Warning Colours

Some animals are poisonous or have a nasty sting. These animals are often brightly coloured to warn other animals to leave them alone.

Milkweed butterfly caterpillars pick up their poisons by eating the leaves of the Milkweed plants. These poisons are passed on to the adults when the caterpillar changes into a butterfly. Many stinging insects, such as wasps and bees, have black and yellow warning colours.

Colourful Males

Male birds of paradise have colourful, spectacular feathers which they show off in a special display to attract a mate. Sometimes they even hang upside down from the tree branches and wave their feathers up and down. The female birds are fairly plain colours and this helps to hide them from enemies when they are sitting on the eggs.

▲ Chameleons can change their colours by changing the size of spots of pigments in the skin. Their colours often match the colours of the trees and bushes they live in and this helps to camouflage them.

Winter Colours

Some animals such as the snow shoe hare live in places where it snows in winter. They grow a white winter coat which helps them to blend into a snowy background. In spring, they grow a darker coloured coat again.

TRUE OR FALSE?

1 If an object reflects all the colours in light, we see white.

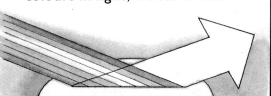

2 Dogs can see in colour.

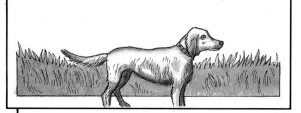

3 Acids turn indicator solutions red.

4 A colour filter stops light of the same colour getting through.

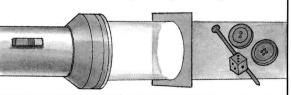

5 Mixing red and green light gives yellow light.

6 Chameleons turn white in winter.

Answers

1 True. If an object absorbs all the colours in light, we see black.

2 False. Dogs, cats, horses and cows cannot see in colour, but birds and monkeys can.

3 True. Alkalis turn indicator solutions blue or green.

4 False. A colour filter lets light of the **same** colour pass through.

5 True. Mixing light is different from mixing paint.

6 False. Chameleons can change colour to match their background, but do not live in snowy places, so do not need to turn white.

Growing Plants

How can you grow new potatoes from old ones? How do you grow plants from stem or leaf cuttings? How do plants spread their seeds? How much water do seeds need to grow? Why do some trees lose their leaves in winter? How can you tell the age of a twig? Why do some kinds of lichen find it hard to grow in polluted air? How can you make your own wild garden?

This section will help you to discover the answers to these questions and has lots of ideas for ways to investigate growing plants.

GROWING PLANTS

In this section, you can discover how to grow plants from cuttings, seeds and bulbs and how the environment affects plant growth.

The section is divided into six different topics. Look out for the big headings with a circle at each end – like the one at the top of this page.

Pages 92–105

Growing New Plants

Bulbs and tubers; stem and leaf cuttings; sprouting seeds; seed dispersal; spores from mosses, mushrooms, ferns and lichens.

Pages 106–114

Water, Light, Air, Warmth

Seeds and water; roots and water; water pipes inside plants; cacti, bottle gardens, growing towards the light; water plants; seasons.

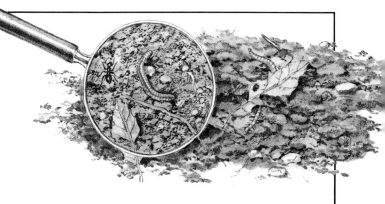

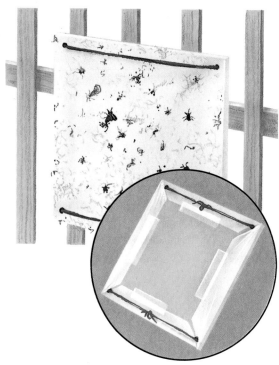

Pages 115–117
Sorting out Soils

Types of soil; leaf litter and rotting leaves; soil erosion.

Pages 118–121
How Trees Grow

Winter buds; measuring tree height; tree rings; bonsai trees.

Pages 122–123
Pollution

Air pollution; lichens and pollution; acid rain.

Pages 124–127
Taking Care of Plants

House plants and holidays, country code; planting trees; making a wild garden.

GROWING NEW PLANTS

Have you ever grown a carrot top? If you put the top of a carrot in a saucer of water, it will sprout leaves. The leaves use the food stored in the carrot to grow. How long does it take for the leaves to appear?

You could also grow tops of other fruits or vegetables, such as pineapples, parsnips or turnips. How are they different from the carrot?

Pineapple top

▼ How many different kinds of bulb flowers can you see in this picture? As each new bulb is exactly the same as its parent, people can grow lots of bulbs which are exactly the same.

Seeds, Bulbs and Cuttings

There are lots of different ways to grow plants. Here are the three main ways.

We can grow some new plants from seeds, which are produced in flowers. Each seed may grow into a new plant that is different from its parent plant.

Some plants grow long, spindly stems and sprout new plants at intervals along the stem. These new plants are identical to their parent plants.

Other new plants grow from pieces of old plants, such as bulbs or cuttings of stems or leaves. These new plants are also identical to their parent plants.

Seeds

Runner

Bulb

Cutting

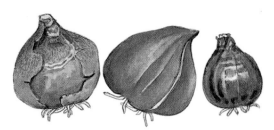

Looking Inside Bulbs

A bulb is an underground stem. It is made up of a flattened stem and a bud surrounded by short swollen leaves. The leaves are full of stored food. In winter, leaves above the ground turn brown and die. Next spring new leaves grow using the food stored in the bulb.

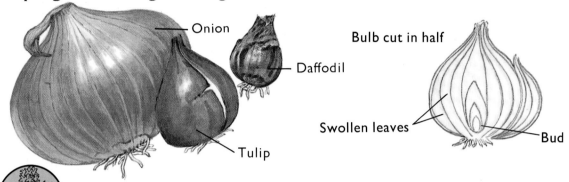

Onion

Daffodil

Tulip

Bulb cut in half

Swollen leaves

Bud

Growing Bulbs

If you grow a bulb such as a hyacinth in water, you will be able to watch the roots develop.

1. Find a jar with a thin neck and fill it with water almost up to the neck. Place the bulb in the neck of the jar.
2. Place the jar in a cool, dark place until you can see a shoot pushing out of the top of the bulb and the roots are about 10 centimetres long.
3. Move the bulb to a warm, light place to finish growing. Make sure the jar is always full of water. How long does it take for the shoot to appear? How long do the roots grow?

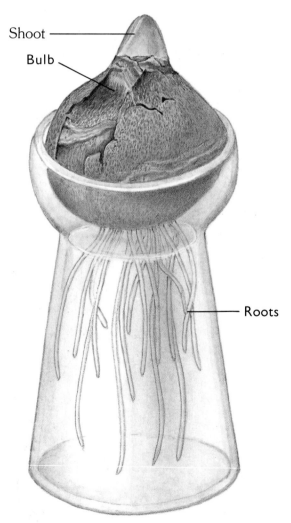

Shoot

Bulb

Roots

Potting Potatoes

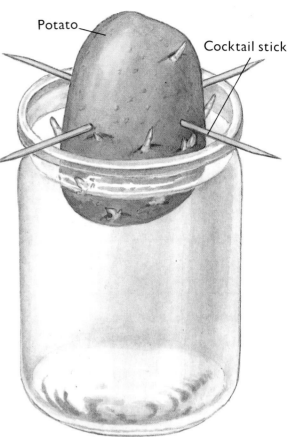

Potato

Cocktail stick

Like bulbs, potatoes are a kind of underground stem. They are called tubers. Tubers store food both to produce new plants and to help the plant survive underground when conditions are not good for growing. The 'eyes' of a potato are really buds, which will sprout into shoots and grow leaves. You can grow several new plants from one potato.

1. Push four cocktail sticks into one end of a potato.
2. Balance the potato over a glass jar full of water. Keep the jar topped up with water.
3. In a few days, shoots will grow from the eyes. Take the potato out of the water and ask an adult to help you cut out each shoot, with a little piece of potato behind it.
4. Plant each shoot in a separate plant pot, covering with soil or potting compost.

Growing Bits of Plants

You will need:

lots of containers (such as old yogurt pots, plastic bottles or mugs, old egg boxes or food trays), soil or potting compost, thin sticks, a trowel, labels, notebook and pencil, plastic bags, elastic bands, scissors, cuttings from different plants (see below).

Plastic bags

Cup

Yogurt pot

Small stick

Labels

Spoon

Pen

How to Take Stem Cuttings

Cut off the tips of side shoots or young stems without flowers in the summer months. This is when plants do most of their growing. Ask an adult to help you make a clean cut just below a leaf node with a pair of scissors or a sharp knife. Make the cuttings about 8–10 centimetres long and strip off the lower leaves. Stand the cuttings in a container of water until they grow roots, then plant them in soil or compost.

Cactus

Geranium cutting

You can also plant offsets which sprout from bigger plants

Spider plant

Place each cutting carefully in a hole.

Water the soil or compost well.

Cover each container with a plastic bag.

1. Make some holes in the bottom of your containers and put a few small stones in the bottom. This helps water to drain away so the soil will not get waterlogged.

2. Fill each container with soil or potting compost.

3. Use the stick to make one or more holes in the soil.

4. Place one cutting carefully in each hole, taking care not to bend or crush the cutting.

5. Put a little more soil around the cuttings. Press the soil down firmly so that the cuttings stand upright.

6. Over a sink or outside, fill the container to the brim with water and let the water drain through.

7. Cover each container with a plastic bag and hold the bag in place with an elastic band (see page 108).

8. After a few days, take off the bag. Keep the soil warm and damp.

9. The cuttings should eventually grow roots and new leaves, but be patient – this won't happen overnight! When some new leaves have grown, transplant each cutting into its own container.

What happens

When you take a cutting from a plant, it can grow new roots and leaves to survive on its own. The parent plant may also sprout new shoots and leaves to replace those you cut off. This is possible because plants (unlike animals) grow all through their lives. Growth is concentrated in certain areas, such as the tips of roots and shoots.

Loads More Leaves

Plants with thick, hairy or fleshy leaves can be grown from leaf cuttings. The best time to take leaf cuttings is from June to September. You will need the same materials as for stem cuttings (see page 96). Plant several leaf cuttings in a pot of damp soil or potting compost. Cover the pot with a plastic bag to keep the air around the cuttings moist. Look at page 108 to see how this works. When the cuttings have sprouted new leaves, separate them carefully, without breaking the roots if possible. Move each cutting to its own pot and leave it in a warm, shady place for a few weeks until it is growing well. How long do your cuttings take to sprout new leaves?

Jade Plants

Jade plants can be grown from just one leaf. Carefully pull a few leaves off a plant and leave them to dry. Then plant the leaves so they just stand up in the soil or compost. They should grow new shoots in a couple of weeks.

African Violets

African violets will also grow from leaves. Ask an adult to help you cut a young, healthy leaf off the plant. Make sure it is a clean cut with some leaf stalk attached. When you plant the stalk, keep the leaf itself clear of the soil.

Jade plant

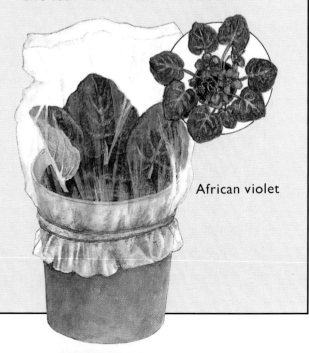

African violet

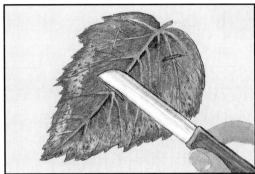

1. Cut main veins under the leaf

2. Weight the leaf down with pebbles

3. New plants sprout from cuts

A New Begonia

With a big enough leaf, you can grow several new plants from one leaf. Begonias can be grown like this. Choose a large, healthy leaf and cut it off the plant. Ask an adult to help you make cuts underneath the leaf on the main veins. Lay the leaf on top of the soil or potting compost with the cut side down. Weight the leaf with some pebbles to keep it near the soil and watch what happens.

How many new plants can you grow from one leaf? How long do they take to grow? Place your cuttings in different places around the room. Does this make any difference to how they grow?

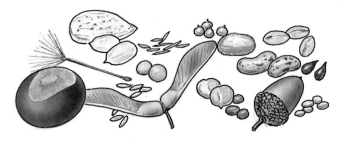

Sorting Seeds

Go on a seed hunt in gardens, hedges, woods and waste ground to make your own collection of seeds. You will also find some seeds in wild bird food or pet food. Do not forget the seeds we eat, such as rice, maize or corn, oats, nuts, beans and peas, nor the seeds inside fruits, such as peaches or apples. How are your seeds the same? How are they different? See how many ways you can find to sort your collection into groups. Here are some ideas: size, weight, wild seeds, seeds from trees or seeds from the farm.

Can you make a picture of some of the different groups of seeds in your collection? Stick the seeds on to coloured card.

Small seeds

As well as measuring seeds with a ruler, you could also see how many will fit into an egg cup or a square 10 centimetres by 10 centimetres.

Mosses, Ferns and Lichens

Mosses, ferns, lichens and fungi do not have flowers so they cannot make seeds. Instead they produce spores, which are very small, simple structures. A spore usually consists of one cell and does not have a

Moss spore case on stalks

Fern spore cases under the leaves

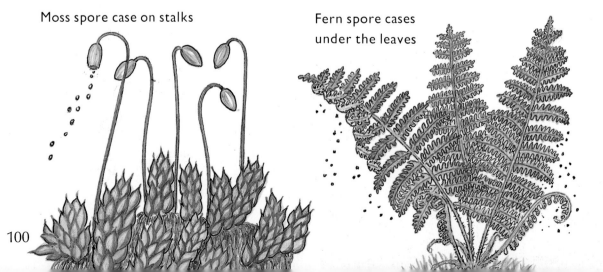

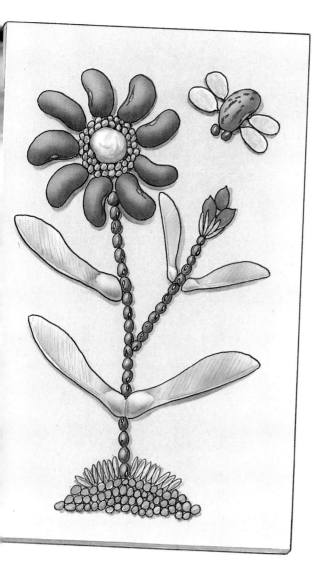

 Mushroom Patterns

The spores of the mushrooms we eat are produced under the cap. To make a spore print, cut off the cap and lay it down on some white paper. Cover the mushroom with a box or a jar to keep out the draughts and leave it overnight. The pattern you will see the next day is made by the spores which fall off the cap.

store of food. If a spore lands in a suitable place, it may grow into a new plant.

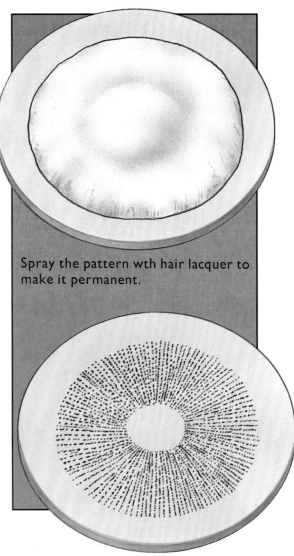

Spray the pattern wth hair lacquer to make it permanent.

◀ Lichen spores may be in discs, cups or spheres

101

Seeds on the Move

Have you ever noticed all the little seedlings growing under a tree? If seeds sprout too close to their parent plant, they will not have enough space, light or water to grow. They stand a better chance of growing and surviving if they move further away.

Some plants have special ways of shooting out their seeds so they land some way away. Squirting cucumber seeds can end up eight metres away from their parent plant. But most seeds rely on the wind, water or animals to move them to a new home.

Seed Quiz

Seeds spread by wind are often small and light with 'wings' or feathery parachutes. Seeds spread by animals may be sticky or have hooks. Some seeds are hidden in fleshy fruits. Seeds spread by water may have large air spaces inside to help them float.

Which of these seeds do you think are spread by the wind, by water or by animals? (The answer is on page 172.)

Burdock

Poppy

Thistle

Willowherb

Nut

Blackberry

Coconut

▲ Some plants hide their seeds inside tasty berries to encourage animals or birds to eat them. These seeds pass through an animal's insides unharmed and grow into new plants.

Grow an Avocado Tree

You can grow unusual house plants from avocados or dates.

1. Stick toothpicks into the side of an avocado stone. This encourages the roots to grow.
2. Balance the stone over a jar of water so that it is just touching the level of the water.
3. When some short roots have grown, take the stone out of the jar and plant it in a container of soil or potting compost (see pages 96–97).

Avocado

Which way is up?

1. Soak some fresh bean seeds in water overnight.
2. Cut a piece of blotting paper to fit around the insides of two large jars with wide necks.
3. Push crumpled paper towels into the middle of the jars.
4. Push a few soaked seeds between the blotting paper and the side of the jar. Place the seeds in different positions – vertical, horizontal and at an angle.
5. Keep the jars in a warm place out of direct sunlight. Water the paper towels regularly to keep the blotting paper moist.
6. After a few days, roots and shoots will start to appear. This is called germination. Which grows first – the roots or the shoots? Which direction do the roots and shoots grow in?
7. When the roots and shoots are a few centimetres long, turn one of the jars upside down. What happens?

What happens
Roots usually grow down because they are attracted by the pull of the Earth's gravity. This strong, invisible force pulls everything towards the middle of the Earth. The shoots always grow upwards towards the light.

Investigating Seeds

Use cocktail sticks to take some different seeds, such as beans, peas or wheat, apart. First peel off the seed skin, called the testa. The testa is a tough waterproof coat which protects the seed. Water gets into the seed through a tiny hole in the testa called the micropyle.

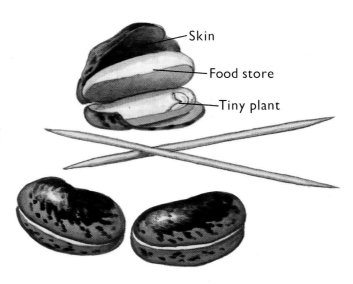

Skin

Food store

Tiny plant

Inside the testa, you should be able to see a tiny plant and one or two seed leaves. A broad bean has two large seed leaves. Which other seeds have two seed leaves? Can you find any seeds with one seed leaf? Sometimes, the seed leaves contain stored food.

Growing Seeds

See if you can measure and compare the growth of different seeds. Cress seeds grow quickly, but runner bean seeds are bigger and easier to measure. Take one of the seeds out every day and measure the roots, shoots and leaves. Mark the edge of a leaf or the tip of a root so you can see where most of the growing is taking place. Do the plants grow all over or just at the edges?

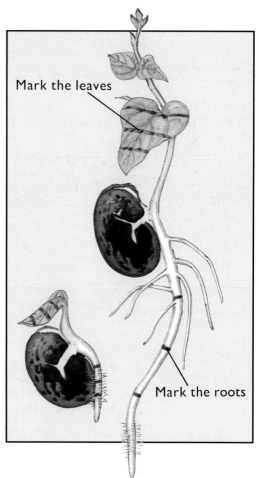

Mark the leaves

Mark the roots

How does the environment around a plant affect the way it grows? Four of the most important factors are water, light, air and temperature. To investigate water, make four equal groups of cress seeds and soak three overnight.

Plants and Water

Seeds

Covers

1

2

3

4

1. In the first container, put some wet seeds on wet cotton wool.
2. In the second container, put wet seeds on dry cotton wool.
3. In the third container, put another group of wet seeds on top of dry cotton wool. Cover the seeds and cotton wool with water. Keep these seeds and those in the first container damp.
4. In the last container, put the dry seeds on top of dry cotton wool. Cover all containers and leave for a few days.

What happens

Seeds need the right amount of water to germinate properly. Dry seeds on dry cotton wool will not grow at all. Wet seeds on dry cotton wool will shrivel up and die. Seeds under water will go rotten. Only wet seeds on wet cotton wool grow well.

Make a clown from modelling clay, leaving a dip in its head. Put damp cress seeds on damp cotton wool in the dip. Watch the clown's hair grow.

 **Roots and Water**

1. Place a clay flower pot full of water in a large bowl.
2. Pack a mixture of soil and sawdust around the pot.
3. Put some soaked peas on the surface of the soil.
4. After a few days, brush the soil off the peas. In which direction are the roots growing?

Flowerpot

Peas

Bowl

What happens

When the only source of water is in the flower pot, the roots grow sideways towards the water. Water is so important to the seeds that the need for water overcomes the pull of gravity.

▼ Rice is planted in fields which are flooded with water. These are called paddy fields. Rice grows well with its roots in lots of water and its shoots in the air.

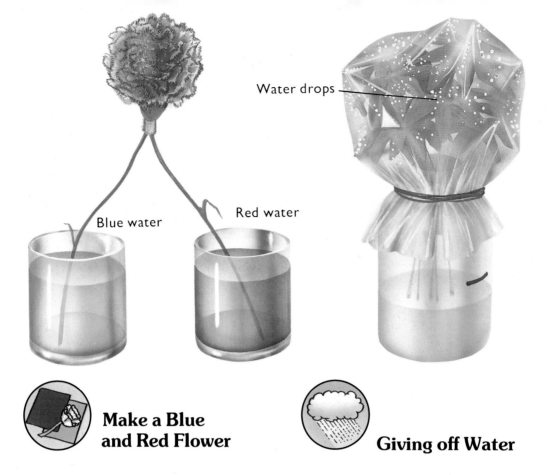

Blue water

Red water

Water drops

Make a Blue and Red Flower

1. Fill one of two clean containers with blue food colouring.
2. Fill the other container with red food colouring.
3. Carefully split the stem of a white carnation from the bottom to the top. Put one half of the stem in the blue water and the other half in the red water.
4. After several hours, some of the petals will turn blue and some will turn red. How long does your flower take to change colour?

What happens
The carnation 'drinks' the coloured water through thin pipes in its stem into the petals.

Giving off Water

1. Fill a large plastic bottle with water and mark the water level.
2. Place a plant in the water and seal the neck of the bottle.
3. Put a plastic bag over the leaves and fix it to the bottle.
4. Leave the plant in the sun for a few days. What happens to the water level? Can you see droplets of moisture on the bag?

What happens
The plant takes up some of the water through its roots. So the water level in the bottle goes down. This water travels up the pipes in the stem and passes out through tiny holes in the leaves.

▲ Cacti have spines instead of leaves, so they do not give off as much water. Spines also collect morning dew and help to shade the plant from hot sun. Animals find it hard to drink water from a plant with spiny prickles. The stems of many cacti, such as saguaros, can expand like a concertina to store water. Their roots spread out in a wide, shallow network to catch as much water as possible when it does rain.

Make a Bottle Garden

Bottle gardens are simple and fun to make and a
very good way to watch plants grow.

You will need:
a large glass or plastic container with a top, gravel, charcoal, potting
compost, a funnel, long sticks, a stick with a cotton reel fixed to the end,
a plastic spoon or fork tied to the end of a garden cane, a sponge on
the end of a stick, small, slow-growing plants such as ferns and mosses.

1. Use the sponge on a stick to clean and dry the container.
2. Put the funnel into the neck of the bottle and pour in a layer of
gravel, then some crushed charcoal and finally dry potting compost.
3. Moisten the compost and pack it down firmly inside the bottle with
the cotton reel on a stick.
4. Use the fork or spoon on a cane to make some small holes in the
potting compost.
5. Use the thin sticks to lower in each plant carefully on to the soil.
6. Put the top on the bottle to seal any moisture inside.
7. Stand the bottle in a bright corner out of direct sunlight. After a day
or so, can you see drops of moisture forming on the sides of the bottle?
8. After a few months, take the top off the bottle to refresh the air and
add a little water if necessary.

If you grow plants in a sealed bottle, they will give off water which will run down the sides of the bottle into the soil. This water can be taken up by the plant again. If the water balance is right, you will not need to water your bottle garden for several months.

 **Follow the Sun**

Did you know that some plants, such as sunflowers, turn to face the Sun as it moves across the sky? Plants use the energy in light to make their food. A green pigment called chlorophyll traps the Sun's energy. Plants are the only living things that can make their own food. All animals have to eat plants – or animals that have eaten plants.

▲ Some plants, such as a Venus fly trap, sometimes trap and eat insects and small animals. They produce digestive juices to break down the meat so they can soak up the goodness.

Make a Potato Maze

1. Make a small hole in a short side of a long cardboard box.
2. Cut out several pieces of cardboard and stick them inside the box to make a maze like the one in the picture.
3. Put a sprouting potato at the end of the box opposite the hole and place the lid on the box.
4. Leave the box in a light place so that light can easily get into the box through the hole in the end.
5. After a few days, take the lid off the box. Has your potato found the pathway through the 'maze' to reach the light?

What happens

The potato senses the light and grows towards it, even though it has to find its way through a maze first. Does your potato shoot eventually grow out of the hole in the side of the box?

Airy Plants

Air is very important to plants. Can you think why we put water weeds in a fish tank?

Cut a short length of pondweed and leave it in a jar on a sunny window-sill. Look carefully at the leaves. Can you see any bubbles in the water? When plants make

Air bubbles

food, they also give off a gas called oxygen. The bubbles given off by the pondweed are bubbles of oxygen. This is the gas that plants and animals, including fishes, need to breathe to stay alive.

Hot and Cold Plants

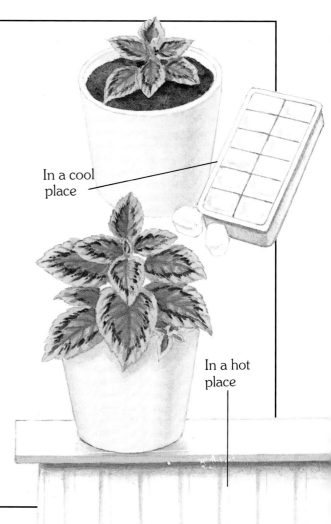

In a cool place

In a hot place

Keep two similar seedlings at different temperatures to see how this affects their growth. Put one in a warm place and one in a cold place. Make sure both seedlings have the same amount of light so they can make food.

Some seeds, such as apple seeds, need a cold period before they will sprout. In the natural world, this means seeds shed in autumn will not grow until warmer weather returns in spring.

Put apple pips in the refrigerator for a few days before planting.

SORTING OUT SOILS

Plants need water and minerals from the soil in order to grow well. There are lots of different kinds of soil, such as clay soil, sandy soil or chalky soil. Some plants only grow well in certain types of soil.

Clay soils hold water and often become waterlogged. In sandy soils, water quickly drains away. In winter, the water in the soil is frozen. Trees with wide, flat leaves cannot draw up enough water to replace that lost from their leaves. So they drop their leaves and rest over the winter.

Collect some soils and see how many differences you can find. What is the texture like? Is the soil smooth, sticky or gritty? Look at the soil carefully with a magnifying glass.

Separating Soil

Make the soil separate by shaking some up in a jar of water and leaving it to soak for a day or two. How many layers can you see? How big are the pieces on the bottom? Are there any bits floating on the surface? Try this investigation again with different kinds of soil.

Humus

Clay

Silt

Sand

Gravel

Rotten Old Leaves

In autumn, look at the rotting leaves under the trees in a wood, a park or a garden. This is called leaf litter. Use a magnifying glass to look at the leaves. How are they different from the leaves on a tree? Can you find any leaf skeletons?

When tree leaves fall to the ground, they are gradually broken into pieces as fungi, bacteria and minibeasts such as worms feed on the leaves. The breakdown of leaves, called decomposition, brings the goodness in the leaves back into the soil to make it rich. Plants can take up the nutrients in the soil and use them to grow.

How Long do Leaves take to Rot?

Collect some leaves from different kinds of tree. Bury the leaves under the soil in a container. Label each leaf and keep the soil moist. Every two weeks dig up the leaves to see how much they have rotted away. You may see fungi feeding as a mass of white threads. Then bury the leaves again. Do some leaves decompose faster than others? Some may take years to rot completely and turn into crumbs. But you can watch the start of the rotting process.

Disappearing Soil

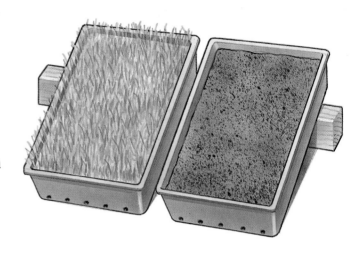

1. Ask an adult to make holes in one end of two seed trays.
2. Fill both trays with soil.
3. Plant grass seeds in one tray. Leave the soil in the other bare.
4. When the grass has grown a few centimetres high, prop the trays up on two blocks of wood, so they are on a slope. Place a bucket below the holes at the end of each tray.
5. Pour the same amount of water, from the same height, into the end of the trays furthest from the holes. How much soil is washed out of each tray?
6. What happens if you make furrows across the tray with bare soil?

▼ Marram grass roots spread in a thick network through the sand. They help to stop sand dunes from being blown away.

Trees grow in two main ways. The twigs and branches grow longer at the tips, so the tree becomes taller and wider. At the same time, the trunk, branches and twigs all grow fatter. Twigs form new buds at the end of the year.

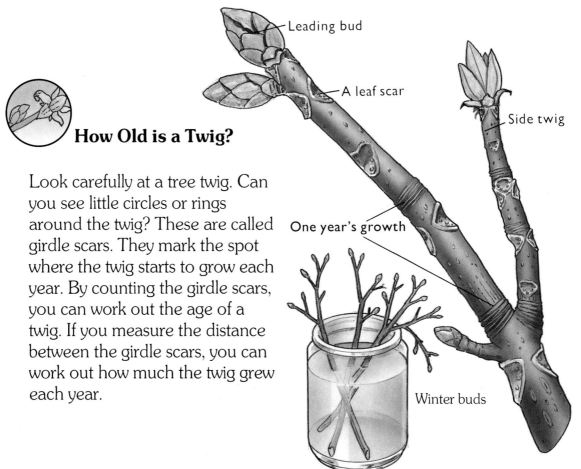

Leading bud

A leaf scar

Side twig

One year's growth

Winter buds

How Old is a Twig?

Look carefully at a tree twig. Can you see little circles or rings around the twig? These are called girdle scars. They mark the spot where the twig starts to grow each year. By counting the girdle scars, you can work out the age of a twig. If you measure the distance between the girdle scars, you can work out how much the twig grew each year.

Growing Buds

The winter buds on a tree contain the beginnings of the shoot, leaves and flowers for the following year. The thick, overlapping scales protect the delicate contents of the bud from cold, from insect attack or from drying out. In spring, bring some twigs indoors and leave them in a jar of water in a warm, sunny place. The best trees to try are horse chestnut ('sticky buds'), willow or birch. The buds may take some weeks to open, but you can watch how the leaves unfold and burst out of the scales.

Trees from Twigs

You can grow trees from small pieces of twig. It is better to pull off the twig, rather than cutting it. Take a small piece of the main twig too. Plant the twig upright in soil or potting compost (pages 96–97) or leave it in a jar of water until it has grown some roots, and then plant it. Try this with willow, poplar or hawthorn trees.

How Tall is a Tree?

Here is a simple way to measure how high a tree has grown. Hold a stick or pencil in front of you, and walk backwards and forwards until the top and bottom of the stick or pencil are level with the top and bottom of the tree. Turn the pencil on its side and ask a friend to walk away from the tree at right angles to you. Stop them when he or she is level with the end of the pencil. You can then measure the distance between the tree and your friend. This distance will equal the height of the tree.

Did You Know?

The largest living thing on Earth is the General Sherman Sequoi Tree in California. It is 83.8 metres tall, and the trunk weighs approximately 1,256 metric tons. Experts believe that this giant tree is over 2500–3000 years old.

▲ Bonsai trees start off as normal trees but do not get enough food and water to grow to their normal size. They are miniatures, and their shoots and roots are pruned to stunt their growth. Bonsai trees can take hundreds of years to grow. If you keep trimming the leaves and shoots of a tree seedling, giving it only a little room to grow, you can make your own bonsai tree.

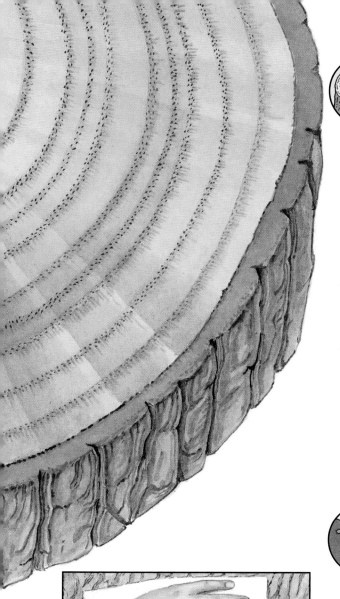

Counting Rings

If you find a tree stump or a pile of cut logs in a plantation, you can work out the age of the trees by counting the rings in the trunk. It is easiest to count the darker rings, showing the end of each year's growth. Measure the width of each ring to see how the amount of growth varies from year to year. If growing conditions are good, the rings will be wider and further apart. Narrow rings show that growth has been slower in those years. Can you think of any reasons why?

Bark Rubbings

The bark of a tree protects it from damage, from drying out or from attack by insects. As the trunk grows, the bark grows, stretches and cracks like skin.

Lay a piece of paper against tree bark and rub over the top with a wax crayon. Don't rub too hard or you will tear the paper. How is the bark of each kind of tree different? How many different kinds of bark can you find? Can you identify trees just by looking at their bark?

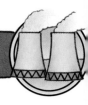

POLLUTION

Plants often find it hard to grow because people have polluted the environment with poisonous waste products from homes, cars, factories or farms.

How Polluted is the Air in your Area?

Make some sticky squares by gluing sticky-backed plastic on to cardboard. Fix them outside in different places. After a few days, look at them with a magnifying glass. How much dirt has each collected? Where are the most polluted places in your area? Where are plants growing best?

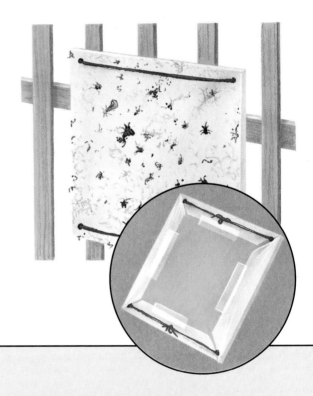

Looking for Lichens

Plants called lichens don't like pollution, such as acid rain. They have no roots and absorb any poisons in the air or water all over their surface. If the poisons build up, they may eventually kill the lichens. Small, flat lichens can cope with highish levels of pollution. So can crusty orange lichens, which grow mostly on stones. But leafy, bushy lichens can survive only in really clean air.

Go on a lichen hunt in your area. Look on walls, roofs, gravestones and tree trunks. Which sort of lichens can you find? The type of lichen will give you a clue to the amount of pollution in your area. If the air is very polluted, you will not find any lichens at all.

▲ Acid rain is formed when poisonous gases from power stations, factories and vehicle exhausts mix with water in the air. Acid rain damages plant growth and weakens the plant. Trees with needles are most likely to be affected.

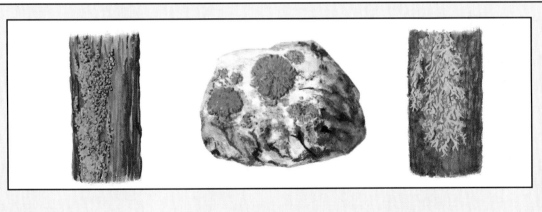

Medium pollution
Grey-green crusty lichens

Medium pollution
Orange crusty lichens

Clean air
Bushy, feathery lichens

TAKING CARE OF PLANTS

Different kinds of plants need different growing conditions. Some plants hate direct sunlight while others grow well in it. Too much water is just as bad for house plants as too little water (see page 106). A good watering once a week is usually better than a few drops every day. House plants need more water in spring and summer.

House Plants and Holidays

When you go on holiday, move your house plants out of the sun and take off any flowers. They use up a lot of water. Here are three ideas for watering your plants while you are away on holiday. Can you think of some more ways?

1. Cover the plant pots with a plastic bag held in place with an elastic band (see page 108).
2. Put several plants in pots in a large bowl of wet newspaper, potting compost or just water. The plants will gradually soak up water through the holes in the bottom of the pots.

3. Fill a container, such as a bucket or an empty ice-cream tub with water. Arrange several plants around the container, but lower down. Hang some lamp wicks from the water container to touch the soil in each pot. The wicks will gradually soak up the water and carry it down to the soil in each pot. The thickness of the wick controls the speed at which the water moves.

▲ All over the world, too many trees are being cut down and not enough planted to take their place. See if you can help to plant more trees in your area. You can also recycle more paper instead of throwing it away. Every tonne of paper that is recycled can save 17 trees.

Country Walks

If you go for a walk in the countryside, be careful not to damage the plants growing there. Remember these points:

✳ Keep to paths and avoid trampling on plants.
✳ Do not pick wild plants. Take photographs or make sketches instead.
✳ Make sure the adults you are with take care with matches, campfires or barbecues. Dry plants catch light easily and fires are hard to put out.
✳ Take litter home with you. It can poison the environment and materials such as plastics may not rot away.
✳ Help to keep the water clean. Don't throw things in streams or rivers.

Making a Wild Garden

Ask an adult to help you make a
patch of ground into an area where
wild plants can grow. The plants will attract insects and wildlife.

Let the grass grow long and allow weeds such as thistles and nettles
to grow in small areas. Caterpillars feed on nettles and many insects,
such as grasshoppers, shelter or lay eggs in the grass.

Clear a patch of soil and sow wild flower seeds just under the surface.
Water the soil to keep it moist. Good seeds to plant are: clover,
cornflower, meadowsweet, scabious, poppies, white campion, bird's foot
trefoil and knapweed.

If there is a fence or wall, you can grow climbing plants such as
honeysuckle or ivy. These will attract insects and provide shelter for
snails. Birds may eventually nest in the tangle of leaves and stems.

Ask an adult to help you build a compost heap where minibeasts can
live and which will provide food for birds.

A Window-Box

If you don't have a patch of ground, you can grow wild plants or herbs in a window-box or a large tray. Keep the soil moist, but not waterlogged. It is best to make some drainage holes in the bottom of the container. Take out some of the plants from time to time so the others will have enough space to grow. Before the plants die back in winter, take some cuttings or collect any seeds ready for next year.

TRUE OR FALSE?

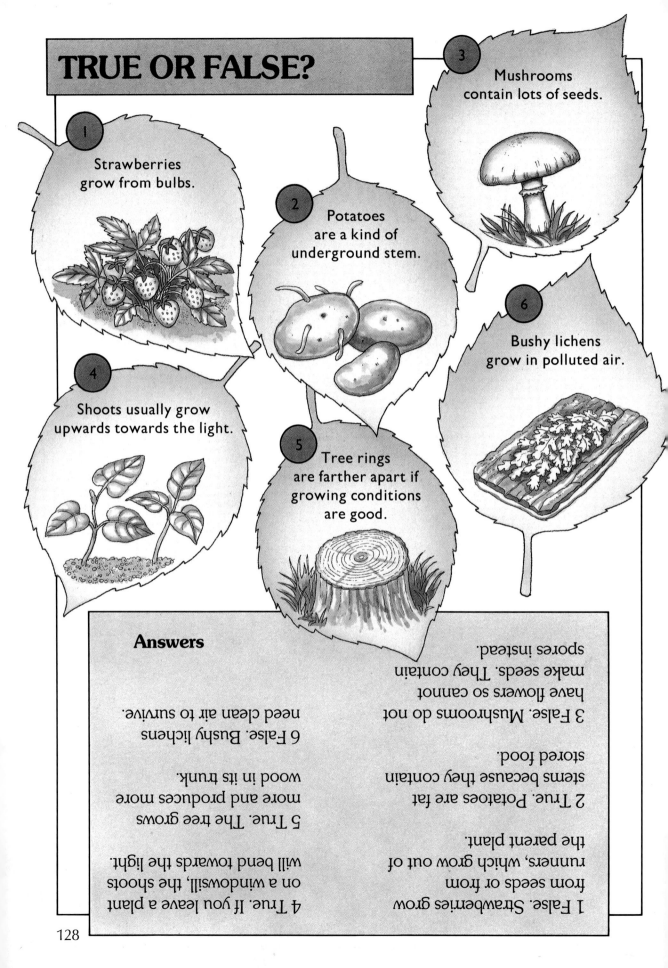

1 Strawberries grow from bulbs.

2 Potatoes are a kind of underground stem.

3 Mushrooms contain lots of seeds.

4 Shoots usually grow upwards towards the light.

5 Tree rings are farther apart if growing conditions are good.

6 Bushy lichens grow in polluted air.

Answers

1 False. Strawberries grow from seeds or from runners, which grow out of the parent plant.

2 True. Potatoes are fat stems because they contain stored food.

3 False. Mushrooms do not have flowers so cannot make seeds. They contain spores instead.

4 True. If you leave a plant on a windowsill, the shoots will bend towards the light.

5 True. The tree grows more and produces more wood in its trunk.

6 False. Bushy lichens need clean air to survive.

Batteries and Magnets

How is a lemon like a battery? How do re-chargeable batteries work? Why is a light bulb filament made of thin wire? What is the difference between a series and a parallel circuit? Why are wires often covered in plastic? How do dimmer switches work? What are magnets made from? Which materials 'stick' to magnets? Why is a compass needle magnetic?

This section will help you to discover the answers to these questions and has lots of ideas for ways to investigate batteries and magnets.

BATTERIES AND MAGNETS

In this section, you can discover how to join batteries, bulbs and wires into simple circuits, more about the pushing and pulling forces around magnets and some of the links between electricity and magnetism.

The section is divided into seven different topics. Look out for the big headings with a circle at each end – like the one at the top of this page.

Pages 132–135

Batteries Everyday

Types of battery; how batteries work; using battery power; making batteries; re-chargeable batteries.

Pages 146–149

Switching On and Off

Making switches; two-way switches; dimmer switches; electrical resistance.

Pages 136–143

Batteries, Bulbs and Wires

How bulbs work; making circuits; series and parallel circuits.

Pages 144–145

Stopping the Flow

Conductors and insulators.

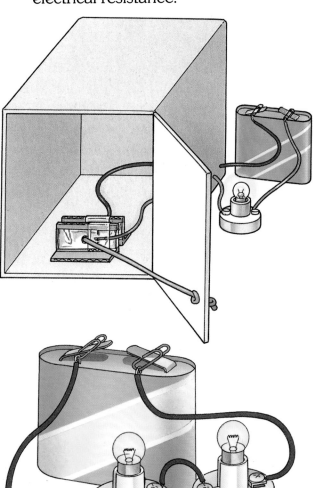

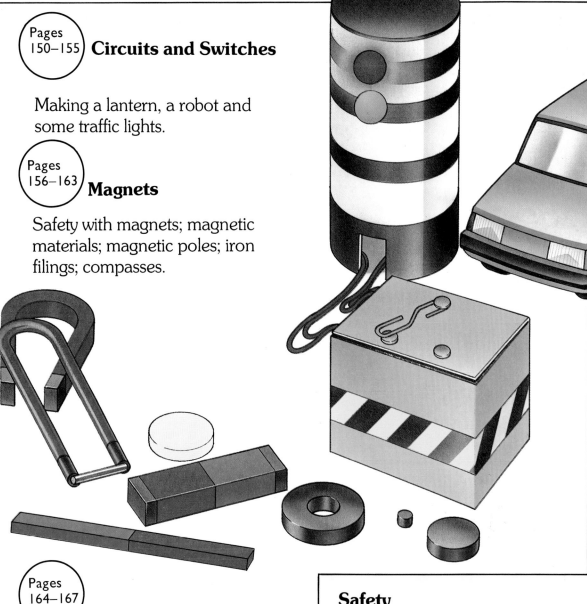

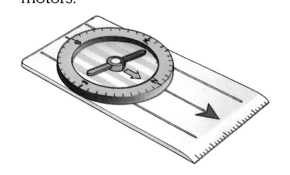

Safety
You should **never** do any experiments with the wires, plugs or sockets in your home or school. The amount of electricity in these things makes them very dangerous. Electric shocks can kill you. Do not go near electricity pylons, overhead cables or sub-stations. Electricity could jump across a gap and kill you.

BATTERIES EVERYDAY

Look carefully around your home, school and in the shops and see how many different batteries you can find. What shapes and sizes are they? Small batteries are used inside watches, hearing aids and pocket calculators. What other things can you think of that use battery power?

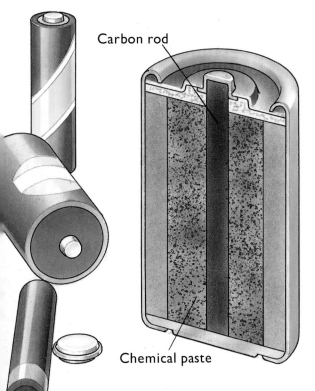

Carbon rod

Chemical paste

Batteries make and store electricity, which is a kind of energy. You cannot see electricity, but you can see that it makes things work. Electricity is made inside a battery by chemicals. Negative electrical charges collect in one part of a battery and positive electrical charges in another. This is shown by the plus and minus signs on a battery. You must **never** take a battery to pieces. The chemicals inside it are dangerous.

Batteries push electricity along wires, and their voltage is the pushing force of the battery. The voltage of batteries, usually printed on the sides, is much less than electricity from a plug or socket on the wall. So batteries are safer to use in investigations. They are also useful because they can be moved from place to place.

▲ How long do the batteries in your toys last before going 'flat'? This happens when chemicals inside a battery are used up. When a battery is worn out, throw it away at once, as chemicals may leak out and cause damage. You should also take batteries out of things you are not going to use for a long time.

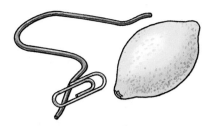

Tongue Tingler

How is a lemon like a battery? This investigation will help you to find out.

Find a short piece of copper wire and a steel paper clip. Poke one end of the wire and the paper clip into the lemon so they are close together but not touching. Touch the free ends of the wire and paper clip on to your tongue. Can you feel a tingle of electricity?

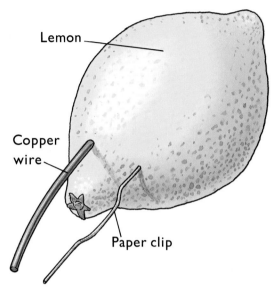

Lemon

Copper wire

Paper clip

What happens

A chemical reaction takes place between the metal wires and the juice inside the lemon. This makes electricity in a similar way to a battery.

Make a Battery

You will need:
clean shiny coins, blotting paper, salt, aluminium foil, thin wire, a small bulb or a meter that measures electricity.

1. Cut up the foil and blotting paper into lots of small squares. Soak the blotting paper squares in salty water.
2. Make a pile of coins, foil and salty blotting paper, keeping the layers in this order. The bigger the pile, the more powerful the battery.
3. To test your battery, put one wire underneath the pile and touch

▲ This car runs on re-chargeable batteries. They do not go 'flat', but can be re-charged to make the chemical reactions start up again.

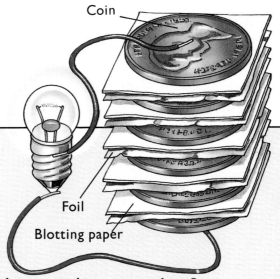

Coin

Foil

Blotting paper

another wire to the top of the pile. If the wires are covered in plastic, the ends must be bare (see page 136).
4. Join the wire to a bulb (see page 137) or a meter. Can you make the bulb light up? How much electricity does your battery produce?

What happens

Chemical reactions in the pile make electricity, which flows along the wires to the bulb or meter.

To find out more about electricity, you can join up batteries, bulbs and wires in lots of different ways. Here are some hints on how to do this.

Wires

Wires are made of metal, which carries electricity, with plastic coating on the outside. The plastic stops the electricity leaking out because it does not carry electricity (pages 144–145). Before you use plastic-covered wire, strip a little plastic off the ends.

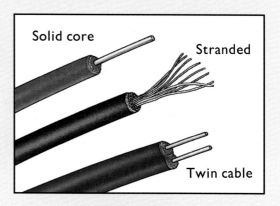

Solid core

Stranded

Twin cable

Batteries

4.5 volt batteries are the most useful for your investigations. It is easier to join wires to batteries with flat ends. The ends of a battery are called terminals. You can use paper clips, crocodile clips or sticky tape to join wires to battery terminals.

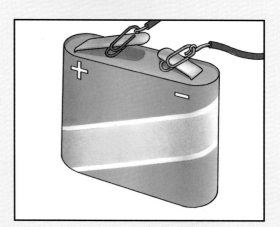

Bulbs

You will need several small, screw-in bulbs – the kind used in torches or bicycle lamps. Use a 2.5 volt or a 3.5 volt bulb with a 4.5 volt battery. Use a 6 volt bulb with a 9 volt battery. You need to touch one wire to the bottom of the bulb and the other wire to the side of the casing.

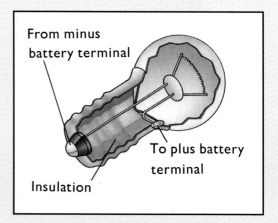

From minus battery terminal

To plus battery terminal

Insulation

▶ A light bulb is a hollow glass shape full of special gas. The glass is attached to a metal tube with wires inside. Electricity flows into the bulb, up one wire, across a coiled wire called a filament, down the other wire and out of the bulb. The filament is made of very thin wire so it is hard for electricity to squeeze through. The way that wire holds back the electricity is called resistance. This makes the filament so hot that it glows and so gives off light.

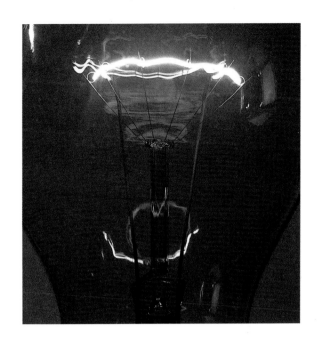

Bulb Holders

When you are doing investigations, it is hard to hold the wires, batteries and bulbs. It helps to fix the bulbs into bulb holders. You can buy these or make some yourself. The pictures show you how to fix the bulb in place.

If you buy one, look at it carefully to see how screws on the side connect up with the two connections on the bulb. To attach the wires to the bulb holder, use a screwdriver to loosen the screws on the sides and fix the wires underneath.

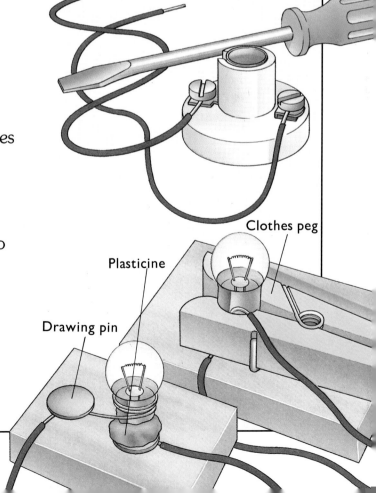

Clothes peg

Plasticine

Drawing pin

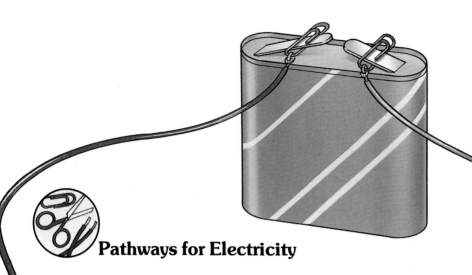

Pathways for Electricity

Can you light up a bulb using a battery and two wires?

1. Fix the bulb firmly in the bulb holder.
2. Clip the end of one wire to the positive battery terminal and fix the other end of the wire to one side of the bulb holder.
3. Join the other wire to the negative battery terminal and the other side of the bulb holder.
4. The bulb should light up. If it does not, check that all the connections are tightly in place.
5. What happens if you use two batteries in series? (Join the negative side of one battery to the positive side of the other).

What happens
Electricity flows from a negative terminal, along the wire, through the bulb and along the other wire to a positive terminal. This pathway along the wire is called a circuit. If the circuit is not properly joined up, electricity cannot flow round the circuit, so the bulb does not light up. When you use two batteries, you have doubled the voltage. Electricity is now pushed around the circuit more strongly, and so the bulb glows more brightly.

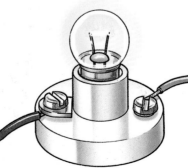

Short Circuits

Do not try to connect one terminal of a battery to the other without putting something like a bulb or a switch (see page 146) into the circuit. The electricity will flow very quickly round and round the short circuit, making the wires hot and the battery run down. With re-chargeable batteries, a short circuit can sometimes make the battery itself heat up and melt.

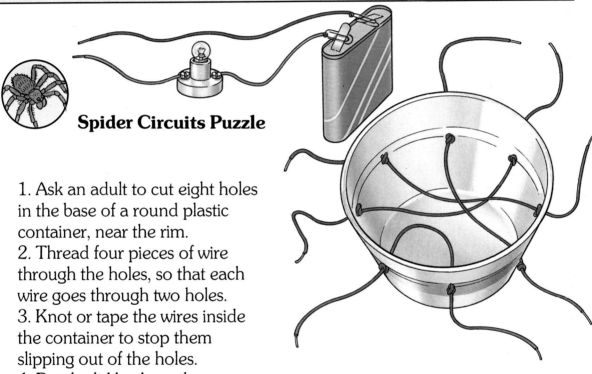

Spider Circuits Puzzle

1. Ask an adult to cut eight holes in the base of a round plastic container, near the rim.
2. Thread four pieces of wire through the holes, so that each wire goes through two holes.
3. Knot or tape the wires inside the container to stop them slipping out of the holes.
4. Put the lid back on the container and decorate it to look like a spider.
5. Give your friends a battery and a bulb in a bulb holder. See if they can work out which pairs of 'legs' go together by making the bulb light up.

What happens
Electricity will only light up a bulb if the circuit is complete. With broken circuits, the bulb will not light.

Make a Quiz Board

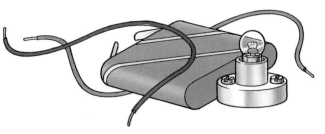

Another way of using circuit tests to solve puzzles is to make a quiz board. Choose any subject you like or know about.

You will need:

a large sheet of thick cardboard, paper fasteners, pens, wire for a simple circuit and wire for the board (or aluminium foil cut into strips), tape or paper, a battery, a bulb in a bulb holder, crocodile clips or paper clips.

Simple circuit

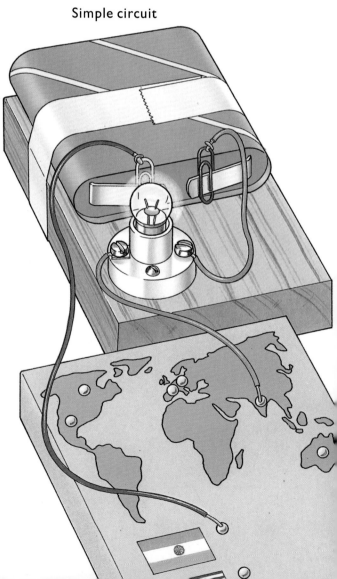

1. Write down or draw some questions and answers on one side of the card. Mix them up, so that questions are not next to the right answers.
2. Push a paper fastener through the board next to each question and each answer.
3. On the other side of the board, use the wire or foil to connect each question with the right answer. Wrap wire or foil round the paper fasteners. If you use foil, put tape or paper between the strips so they do not touch.
4. Make a circuit with the battery, bulb and wires (page 138). Leave the bare ends of the wires free.
5. Touch one wire to a paper fastener next to a question and the other wire to a paper fastener next to the answer you think is

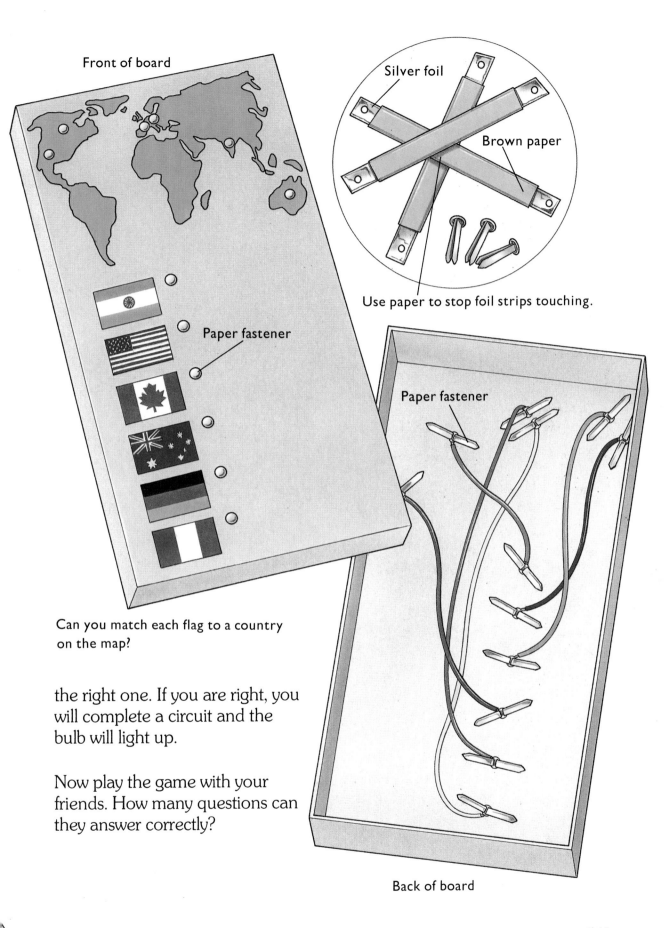

Front of board

Silver foil

Brown paper

Use paper to stop foil strips touching.

Paper fastener

Paper fastener

Can you match each flag to a country on the map?

the right one. If you are right, you will complete a circuit and the bulb will light up.

Now play the game with your friends. How many questions can they answer correctly?

Back of board

141

Single or Double Circuits

If you link more than one bulb into the same piece of wire, the same electricity will go through each bulb. So several bulbs will glow more dimly than one bulb on its own. If you take one bulb out, you break the circuit and the other bulbs will go out too. This kind of single circuit is called a series circuit.

There is another way of wiring more than one bulb into a circuit. In a parallel circuit, each bulb has its own circuit. If it has two bulbs, each bulb glows more brightly. If you take one bulb out, the other bulb stays on.

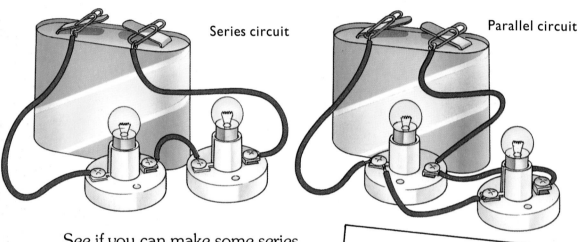

Series circuit

Parallel circuit

See if you can make some series and parallel circuits. You could do some drawings like these to show how the batteries, bulbs and wires are arranged in your circuits.

The wiring in a house is usually arranged on a parallel circuit. If you switch off one light, the other lights stay on.

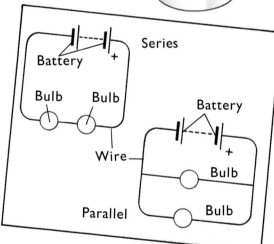

Battery

Series

Bulb   Bulb

Wire

Battery

Parallel

Bulb

Bulb

▶ Christmas tree lights are often wired up on a series circuit.
If one bulb stops working the rest of the bulbs go out too.
Can you think what else might use a series circuit?

STOPPING THE FLOW

Which materials does electricity flow through? Make a collection of materials to test, such as paper, metal objects (keys, forks and coins), cloth, plastic, a stone, a rubber, cork and wood.

Make a circuit with a battery, a bulb and two wires. Leave the ends of the wires free. Use each object in turn to complete the circuit. Does the bulb light up? Sometimes the paint on objects stops the electricity flowing through. Scratch a little paint off the surface to see if it makes any difference.

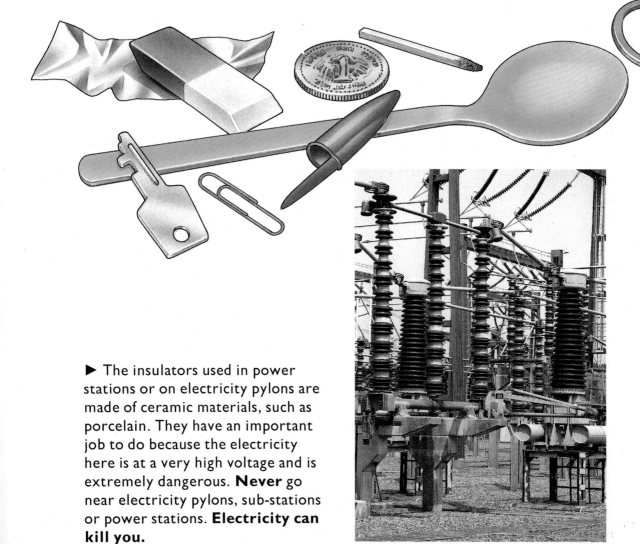

▶ The insulators used in power stations or on electricity pylons are made of ceramic materials, such as porcelain. They have an important job to do because the electricity here is at a very high voltage and is extremely dangerous. **Never** go near electricity pylons, sub-stations or power stations. **Electricity can kill you.**

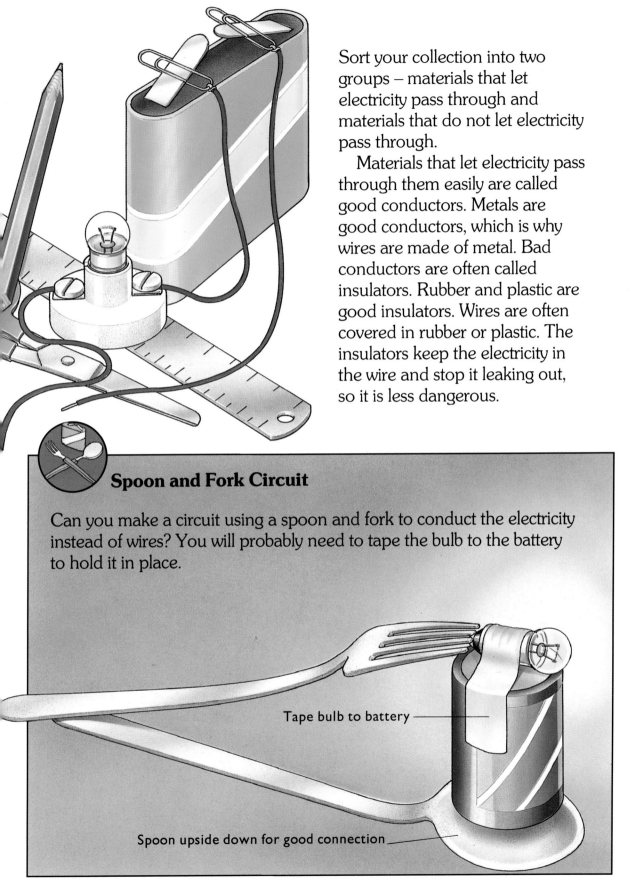

Sort your collection into two groups – materials that let electricity pass through and materials that do not let electricity pass through.

Materials that let electricity pass through them easily are called good conductors. Metals are good conductors, which is why wires are made of metal. Bad conductors are often called insulators. Rubber and plastic are good insulators. Wires are often covered in rubber or plastic. The insulators keep the electricity in the wire and stop it leaking out, so it is less dangerous.

Spoon and Fork Circuit

Can you make a circuit using a spoon and fork to conduct the electricity instead of wires? You will probably need to tape the bulb to the battery to hold it in place.

Tape bulb to battery

Spoon upside down for good connection

We use good conductors to make switches. When a switch is off, there is a gap in a circuit so electricity cannot flow. When a switch is on, the gap is closed up to complete the circuit. Electricity can flow right round the circuit to make something work.

Switches are very useful in investigations with batteries, bulbs and wires. Here are some ideas for different ways to make switches:

Paper Clip
Use a paper clip to link two drawing pins. When you move the clip away from one pin, you break the circuit and turn the switch off. You could use card wrapped in foil instead of a paper clip.

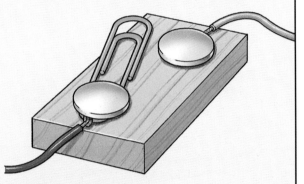

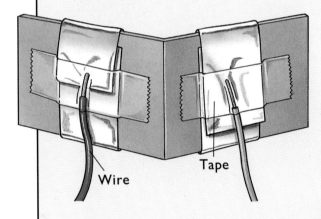

Tape

Wire

Folded Card
Wrap foil around the ends of a piece of folded card. When the folded card presses the two pieces of foil together, it completes the circuit and turns the switch on. This is a kind of pressure switch.

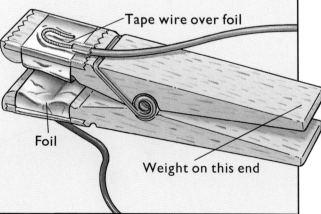

Tape wire over foil

Foil

Weight on this end

Clothes Peg
Wrap the ends of a clothes peg in foil. A weight pressing on the other end turns the switch off. If the weight is taken away, the foil ends spring together and turn the switch on.

Make a Burglar Alarm

You will need:
A large box to make a 'safe', a battery, a bulb or buzzer, cardboard, foil, scissors, sticky tape, string, wire or thread, coloured pencils, treasure for your 'safe'.

1. Cut two pieces of card and wrap them in foil.
2. Fix one wire to each piece of card with tape.
3. Cut two small holes in the side of the box and push the wires through from the inside.
4. Make a circuit outside the box with the battery, the wires and the bulb.
5. Use string or wire to join both pieces of card to the door, as in the picture. Arrange the pieces of card in the 'safe', so that they are not touching.
6. Decorate your 'safe', put some treasure inside and close the door.

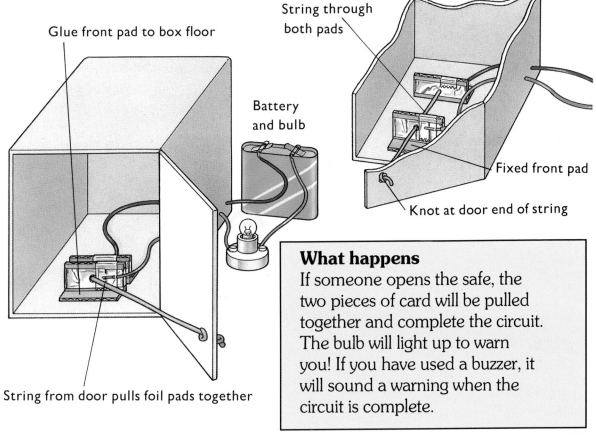

Glue front pad to box floor

String through both pads

Battery and bulb

Fixed front pad

Knot at door end of string

String from door pulls foil pads together

What happens
If someone opens the safe, the two pieces of card will be pulled together and complete the circuit. The bulb will light up to warn you! If you have used a buzzer, it will sound a warning when the circuit is complete.

Make a Two-way Switch

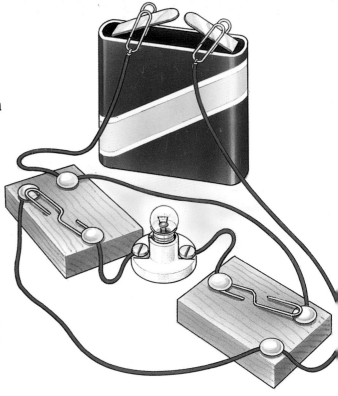

Do you know of a light that can be switched on or off from different places? This needs a special kind of switch called a two-way switch.

You will need to make two switches (see page 146) and wire them into a circuit like the one in the picture.

You should find that the bulb can be turned on or off using either one of the switches to break a circuit or complete a circuit. In a building, much longer wires connect the two switches together in a similar way.

Make a Dimmer Switch

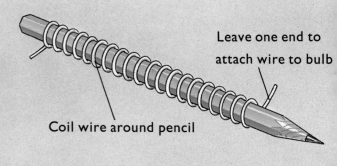

Leave one end to attach wire to bulb

Coil wire around pencil

You will need:
a battery, a bulb, two pieces of plastic-covered wire, a piece of bare wire, a pencil.

1. Coil the bare wire round and round the pencil.
2. Make a circuit with the battery, bulb and plastic-covered wires.
3. Twist the end of one of the plastic-covered wires around the end of the coiled wire.
4. Touch the end of the other plastic-covered wire to the coiled wire at different points. Does the brightness of the bulb change?

▲ Resistors, such as the ones on this circuit board, change the flow of electricity. They are used in light dimmer switches and volume controls.

What happens

When a lot of the bare, coiled wire is in the circuit, the electricity has to push hard through the wire. There is a lot of resistance, so the bulb is dim. If a shorter length of coil is in the circuit, there is less resistance to the electricity. More energy is left to light the bulb, so it glows more brightly.

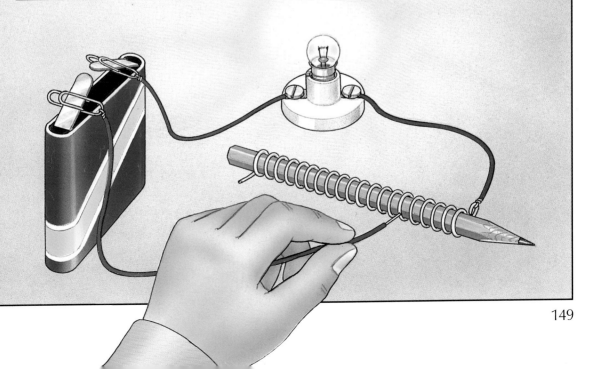

On the next six pages are some ideas for things to make using circuits and switches. How many more ideas can you think of?

 Make a Lantern

You will need:

a small cardboard box, a bulb holder, a small bulb (2.5 or 3.5 volts), a 4.5 volt battery, a switch (page 18), 2 pieces of wire about 50 cm long, 1 piece of wire about 10 cm long, coloured cellophane, sticky tape, scissors, screwdriver.

1. Cut a large, square hole in three sides of the box. Make a round hole in the fourth side big enough to take two pieces of wire.

2. Glue the cellophane over each of the square holes in the sides of the box.

3. Screw the bulb into the bulb holder and join one piece of the long wire to each side of the bulb holder.

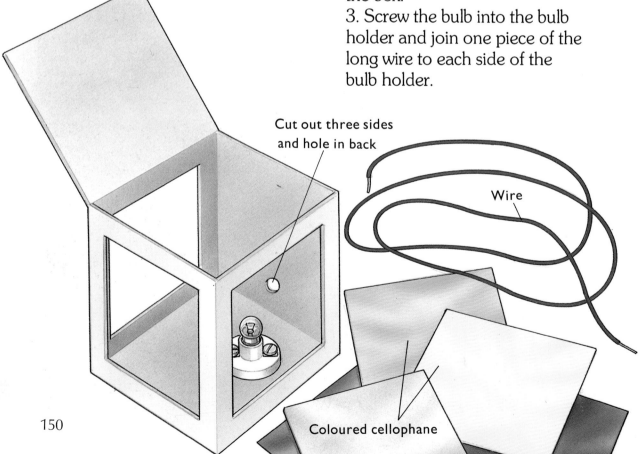

Cut out three sides and hole in back

Wire

Coloured cellophane

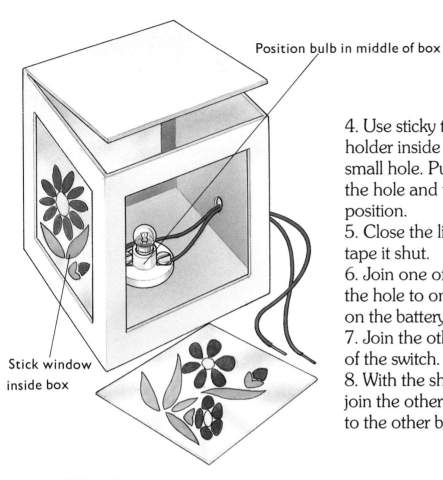

Position bulb in middle of box

Stick window inside box

4. Use sticky tape to fix the bulb holder inside the box, close to the small hole. Pull the wires through the hole and tape them in position.
5. Close the lid of the box and tape it shut.
6. Join one of the wires from the hole to one of the terminals on the battery.
7. Join the other wire to one side of the switch.
8. With the short piece of wire, join the other side of the switch to the other battery terminal.

What happens
When you turn on the switch, you complete the circuit and make the light come on. To make the light flash, you can flick the switch on and off.

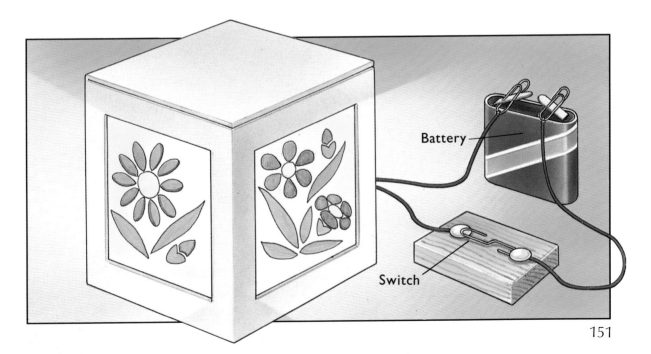

Battery

Switch

Make a Robot

1. Cut away one side of one of the cardboard boxes. Make two small holes with the scissors in the opposite side of the box. This will be the front of the robot's head.

You will need:
4 large cardboard boxes, 4 cardboard tubes, aluminium foil, sticky tape, glue, a 4.5 volt battery, 2 bulbs (3.5 volts), 2 bulb holders, a switch (page 9), 2 long pieces and 2 short pieces of wire, screwdriver, scissors.

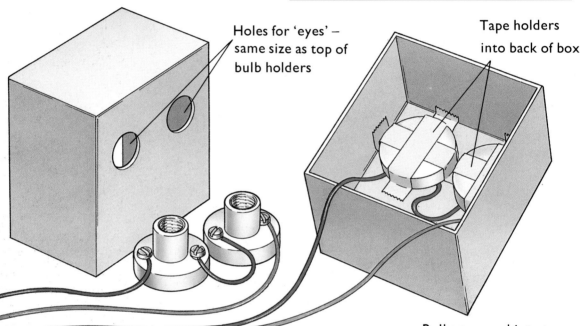

Holes for 'eyes' – same size as top of bulb holders

Tape holders into back of box

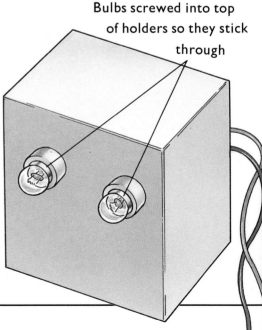

Bulbs screwed into top of holders so they stick through

2. Screw the bulbs into the bulb holders. Join the holders together with a short piece of wire.
3. Fix a long piece of wire to the other side of each bulb holder.
4. Carefully push the bulbs through the holes in the box. Tape or glue them in place inside the box.

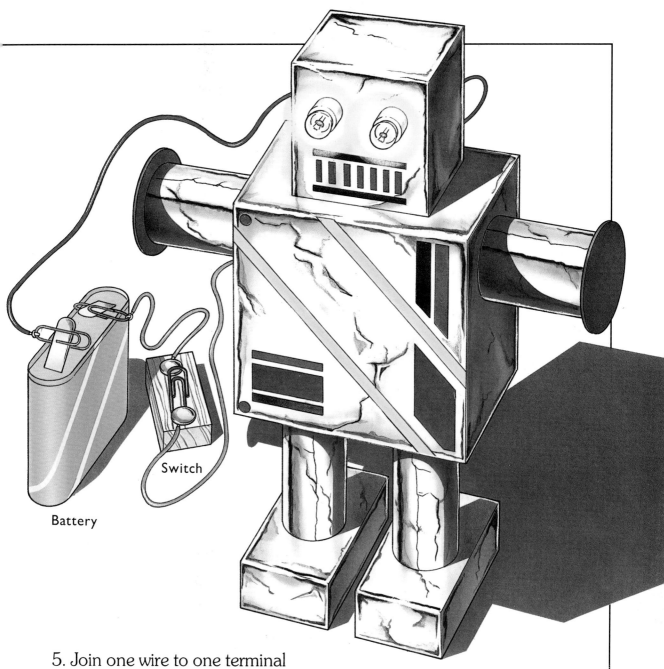

Switch

Battery

5. Join one wire to one terminal
on the battery and the other wire
to one side of the switch.
6. Join the switch to the other battery terminal with the short piece
of wire.
7. Glue or tape the other boxes and tubes to the head to make the
body, arms and legs of the robot.
8. Cover the robot with foil and any other decorations that you like.
9. Flick the switch on and off to complete the circuit and make the
robot's eyes flash.

Make some Traffic Lights

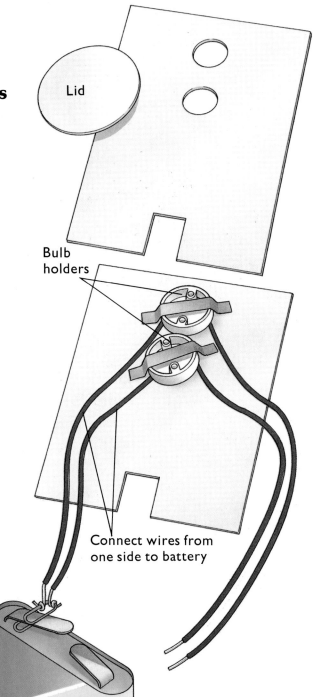

Lid

Bulb holders

Connect wires from one side to battery

1. Cut two holes towards the top of the thin cardboard. Make the holes one below the other. Cut another hole in the bottom edge of the card directly underneath the two holes.
2. Paint one bulb red and the other bulb green. Screw the bulbs into the bulb holders.
3. Join one long piece of wire to each side of the bulb holders. Push the bulbs through the holes in the card. Tape the back of the holders in place.
4. Join one of the wires from each bulb holder to a battery terminal. Put the battery in the box.
5. Push two paper fasteners through the box lid. Bend back the prongs to keep them in place.
6. Join the free wire from one bulb holder to one paper fastener and the free wire from the other holder to the other paper fastener.

You will need:
2 bulb holders, 2 bulbs (3.5 volts), a 4.5 volt battery, 4 long pieces of wire at least 50 cm long, 1 short piece of wire about 10 cm long, 3 paper fasteners, 1 paper clip, a small cardboard box, thin cardboard, red and green poster paints, screwdriver, scissors, tape or glue, paper, paints for decoration, modelling clay.

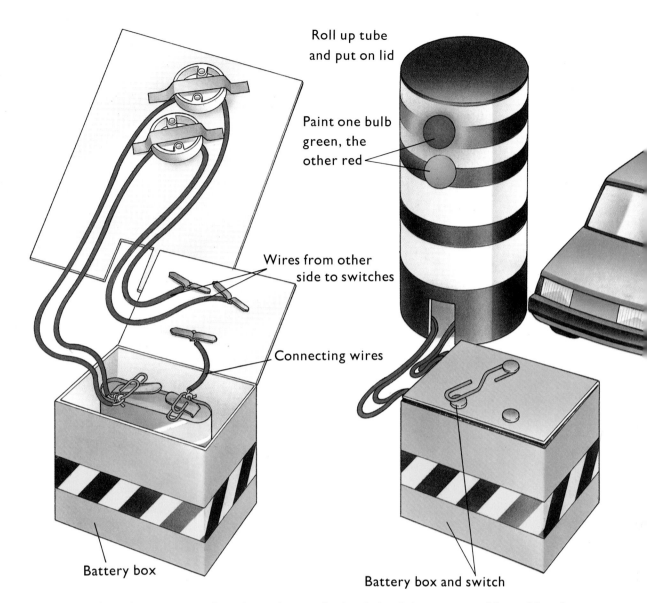

Roll up tube
and put on lid

Paint one bulb
green, the
other red

Wires from other
side to switches

Connecting wires

Battery box

Battery box and switch

7. Push a third paper fastener through the lid of the box and bend back the prongs. Join this paper fastener to the other battery terminal with a short piece of wire. On top of the box, bend a paper clip around this fastener. The paper clip must be able to touch both the other paper fasteners.

8. Close the lid of the box and tape it shut.

9. Roll the thin card into a tube around the bulb holders. Tape the tube sides in place. Pull the wires out through the bottom.

10. Stand the tube upright in modelling clay.

11. Tape a paper circle to the top of the tube, so you cannot see the wiring inside.

12. When the paper clip touches each paper fastener, it completes a circuit and makes the red or green light come on. When you move the paper clip, the lights change.

MAGNETS

Have you got a magnet? What shape is it? Magnets come in all sorts of shapes and sizes, from long, thin ones to the round ones on refrigerator magnets. See how many shapes and sizes you can find.

Magnets are very useful for sticking things together without using glue. They are used to keep the doors of refrigerators shut. They are also used to hold the pieces on the board in travel games. Can you find any other uses for magnets?

Safety with Magnets

Magnets can damage watches, televisions, computer discs, videos and tape recorders. Make sure you keep magnets well away from these things.

▶ The first magnets were made more than 2000 years ago from lodestone, a special black stone which pulls iron materials towards it. It contains an iron ore called magnetite. Nowadays, most magnets are made from iron or steel.

156

Magnetic Materials

Magnets have the power to pull some materials, called magnetic materials, towards them. To see what is magnetic, collect objects made from different materials, such as paper, wood, metal, plastic, glass and rubber.

Which objects 'stick' to your magnet? Can you feel the pull of the magnet through your fingers?

Sort your collection into magnetic materials and non-magnetic materials. To keep a record of your results, you could draw a chart.

 Pulling Power

How strong are magnets? Does the shape or size of a magnet affect its strength?

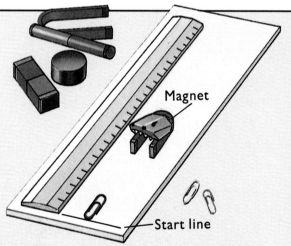

Collect together different magnets and mark a scale on a piece of paper. Place a paper clip at one end of the scale and slide each magnet along the scale from the other end. Mark where the magnet starts to pull the paper clip towards itself. Are bigger magnets stronger than smaller ones?

Stopping the Power

Can some materials block the pulling power of a magnet? See if your magnet still works through glass, paper or wood.

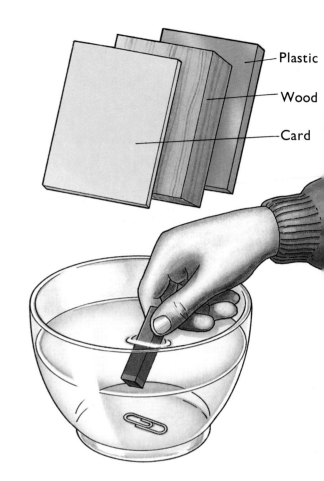

Plastic

Wood

Card

Drop a paper clip into a bowl of water. Can you use a magnet to pick up the paper clip without getting your fingers wet?

Magnetic Maze

1. Draw a maze on one side of a paper plate.
2. Ask a friend to hold the plate for you.
3. Put a paper clip at the start of the maze and hold a bar magnet under the plate.
4. Time how long it takes to pull the paper clip through the maze without touching any of the lines. Have a race with your friend. Who has the steadiest hand?

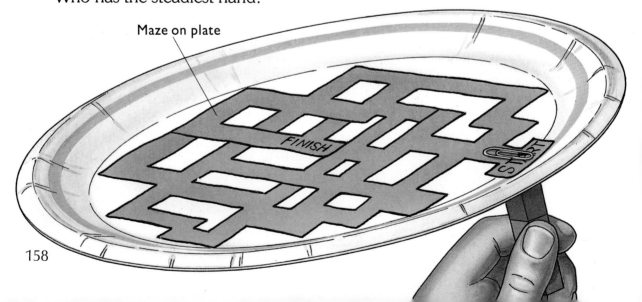

Maze on plate

FINISH

START

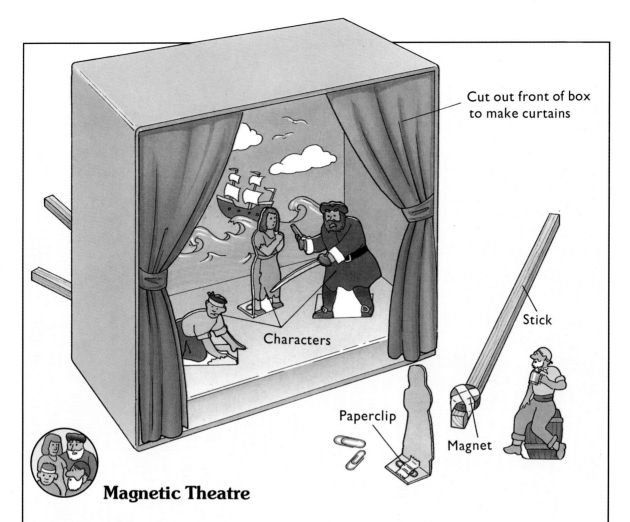

Cut out front of box to make curtains

Stick

Characters

Paperclip

Magnet

Magnetic Theatre

You will need:

thick cardboard, thin card, scissors, paint or crayons, sticky tape, glue, thin sticks, a cardboard box, small magnets.

1. Draw and cut out a model theatre stage from thick cardboard. Colour the scenery and curtains with the paints or crayons.

2. Cut away the top of the box. Turn the box on its side and glue the stage to the bottom and sides. Leave about 4 centimetres space under the stage. Cut away the bottom of the box below the level of the stage. Stick it at the front to hide the gap.

3. Draw and colour in your actors on thin card. Cut them out, with a piece of card at the bottom. Bend this back so they stand up.

4. Tape a paper clip on the bent card behind each actor.

5. Tape a magnet to each of the thin sticks.

6. Put the actors on stage. Slide the magnetic sticks in through the cut bottom of the box, so they are under the stage. Move the actors with the magnets.

 **Pull and Push**

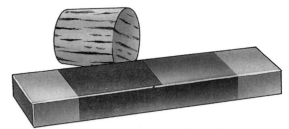

The pulling force of a magnet is strongest at certain points, called the poles of the magnet. In a long, straight bar magnet, the poles are at either end of the magnet. They are called the North and South Poles (you can find out why on page 162). The poles of one magnet do not always pull the poles of other magnets towards them. Sometimes they push them away. This investigation will show you more about how magnets behave.

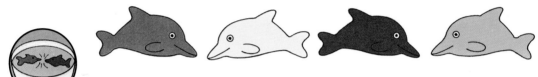

Magnetic Dolphins

1. Draw two dolphin shapes on cardboard. Cut them out.
2. Glue or tape bar magnets to two corks and stick a dolphin on top of each cork and magnet.
3. Float the dolphins in a bowl of water. What happens when you push the dolphins together?
4. Turn one of the dolphins around. What happens?

What happens
The dolphins stick together if the magnets are one way round. But when you turn one magnet around, it will push the other dolphin away. Two North Poles or two South Poles will push each other apart, but a North Pole and a South Pole will stick together. Magnets will stick together if the poles are different, and will push each other apart if the poles are the same.

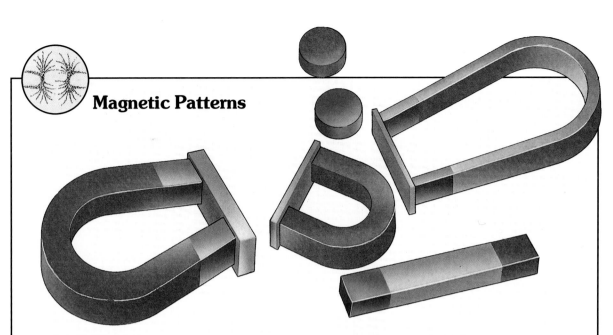

Magnetic Patterns

Round magnet: poles around edge

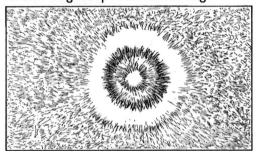

Horseshoe magnet: poles at end

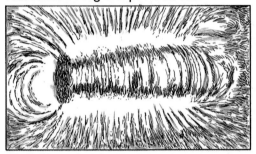

Bar magnet: different poles (at ends) pull together

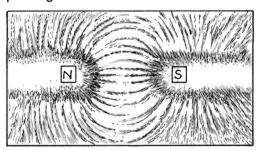

Bar magnet: same poles (at ends) push apart

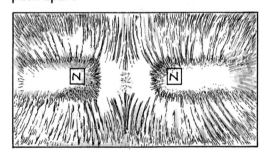

We cannot usually see the pushing and pulling forces around a magnet. But by scattering some iron filings on a piece of paper and placing a magnet under the paper, some of the lines of force become clear. Where the magnet gives out a strong force, lots of iron filings group together. Where the force is weaker, the filings are further apart.

With two poles that are the same, the filings show that the poles are pushing apart. With two poles that are different, the filings show how the poles pull together.

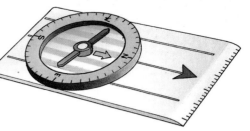

Pointing North and South

If you hang a magnet up by a thread or float it on water, it spins slowly. When it comes to rest, it points towards the North and South Poles of the Earth. (This is why magnets are said to have North and South Poles.) The Earth itself has magnetic powers and is like a giant magnet. The Earth's huge magnetic force pushes and pulls smaller magnets. Did you know that a compass needle is a magnet?

To find out more about magnets, make one yourself.

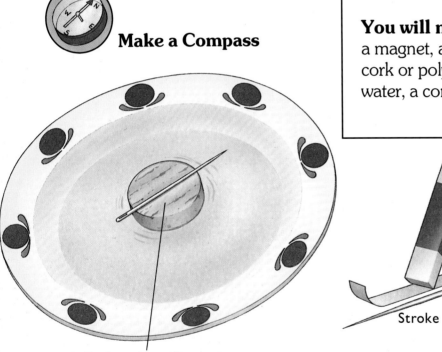

Make a Compass

> **You will need:**
> a magnet, a needle, a piece of cork or polystyrene, a bowl of water, a compass.

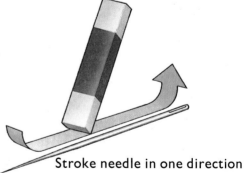

Stroke needle in one direction

Cork with needle on top

1. Stroke the end of the magnet along the needle about 50 times. Stroke it in the same direction each time and hold the needle away after each stroke. This will turn the needle into a magnet.
2. Put the needle on top of the cork or polystyrene and float it in the bowl of water.
3. Place a compass next to the bowl of water and check that your needle points in the same direction as the compass needle.

▲ Lodestone (meaning 'the stone that leads') was used to guide people centuries ago. Nowadays, magnetic compass needles are used on ships and aeroplanes as well as on land to help people find their way.

Did you know that you can make magnets with electricity? When electricity flows along a wire, it makes the wire magnetic. You can test this by building a circuit with a switch. Put a compass near the wire and watch to see what happens to the compass needle when you switch on the electricity.

What happens

The magnetic force in the wire will push and pull the magnetic compass needle and make it swing about.

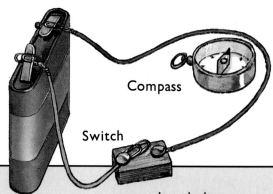

Compass

Switch

Make an Electro-magnet

If a wire carrying electricity is wound into a coil, it produces a stronger magnetic force than a straight wire. And if an iron bar is placed inside the coil of wire, the magnetic force is stronger still. Make an electro-magnet to see how this works.

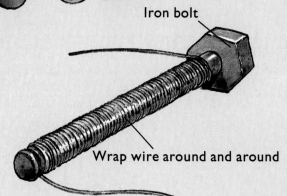

Iron bolt

Wrap wire around and around

1. Wind the long piece of wire round the bolt, keeping the coils close together. The more times you wind the wire round the bolt, the stronger the magnet.
2. Join one end of the wire to a battery terminal and the other end of the wire to the switch.

You will need:

a large iron bolt, a nail, 2 metres of wire, a short piece of wire, a switch, a battery, paper clips, a matchbox, a wooden frame, thread.

▲ This electro-magnet is sorting scrap metals from other non-magnetic materials. Electro-magnets are useful because they only work when electricity is switched on.

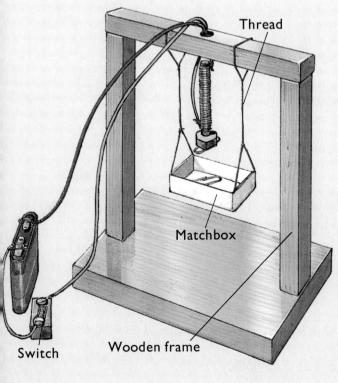

Thread

Matchbox

Switch

Wooden frame

3. Use the short piece of wire to join the other side of the switch to the battery terminal.
4. When the electricity is on, how many paper clips can the bolt pick up? How far away can it attract a clip hanging from some thread?
5. Hang a matchbox from a wooden frame, with your bolt hanging above it. Turn on the electricity, so a paper clip sticks to the bolt. Swing the matchbox and turn off the electricity. Can you catch the clip in the box?

▲ In a bicycle dynamo, a magnet moves when the wheel turns and produces electricity. This makes the bicycle lamp come on. When the cyclist stops pedalling, the magnet stops moving. No electricity is produced, so the lamp goes out. Dynamos use magnets and movement to make electricity.

Making Things Move

An electric motor works in the opposite way to a dynamo. It uses magnetism and electricity to produce movement. Make a motor yourself to see how they work.

1. Ask an adult to push a knitting needle through two corks, one large and one small.
2. Wind some copper wire about ten times round the large cork. Tape the ends to the smaller cork.

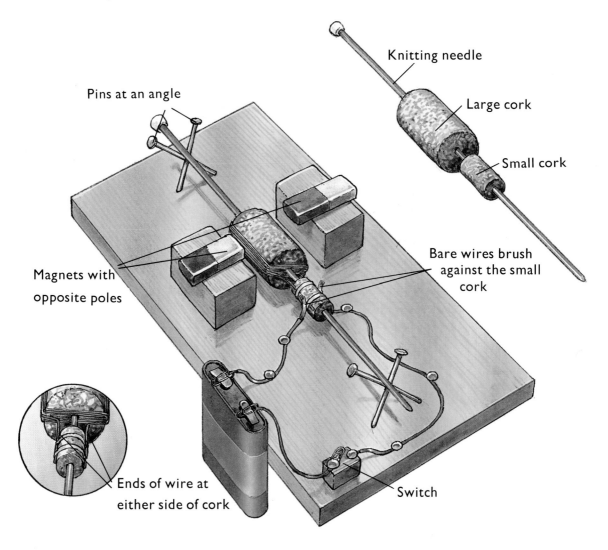

Knitting needle

Large cork

Small cork

Pins at an angle

Bare wires brush
against the small
cork

Magnets with
opposite poles

Ends of wire at
either side of cork

Switch

3. Push some pins into a wooden board and balance the knitting needle on the pins. Make sure the corks can turn freely as the needle turns.

4. Balance two bar magnets on top of wooden blocks either side of the cork.

5. Make a circuit with a battery, some short wires and a switch. Fix the short wires to the board with drawing pins.

6. Touch the bare ends of the battery wires to the wires taped on the small cork. When you turn on the switch, the corks should turn round.

What happens
When electricity passes through the coils of wire around the large cork and back to the battery again, it makes the wire magnetic. When this magnetic force meets the magnetic force between the two magnets, it makes the cork turn round.

TRUE OR FALSE?

1 Batteries push electricity along wires.

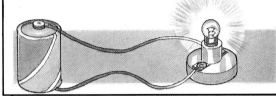

2 Electricity will only light up a bulb if a circuit is complete.

3 If you take one bulb out of a parallel circuit, the other bulbs will go out.

4 Plastics are good at conducting electricity.

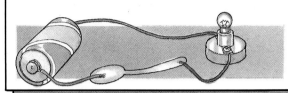

5 The same magnetic poles attract each other.

6 A compass needle is a magnet.

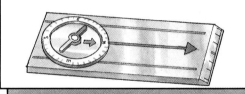

Answers

1 True. This is called the voltage of the battery and it is much less than the voltage of mains electricity.

2 True. If there is a gap in a circuit, electricity cannot make the bulb light up.

3 False. In a parallel circuit, each bulb has its own circuit. If you take one bulb out, the others stay on.

4 False. Plastics are not good conductors. They are used to insulate wires and stop the electricity leaking.

5 False. Different magnetic poles attract each other.

6 True. Compass needles point to the Earth's magnetic North and South Poles.

GLOSSARY

Acid A sour substance which is the chemical opposite of an **alkali**. It contains hydrogen and can be replaced by metals.

Acid rain Rain that is more acidic than normal because it has chemicals from vehicle exhausts, power stations and factories dissolved in it.

Aerofoil A wing that is curved on top and flat underneath.

Aileron Flaps on the wings of an aeroplane that can be moved up and down to make the aeroplane turn left or right.

Air pressure The effect caused by the **weight** of all the air in the **atmosphere** pressing down on everything on Earth. Low air pressure usually brings bad weather and high air pressure usually brings good weather.

Alkali The chemical opposite of an **acid**. An alkali neutralizes an acid to produce a salt and water.

Atmosphere The layer of invisible gases around the Earth. It is made up mainly of **oxygen** and nitrogen.

Barometer An instrument for measuring **air pressure**.

Bulb A short underground stem wrapped in swollen, fleshy leaf bases.

Chlorophyll The **pigment** in plants which makes them look green. Chlorophyll traps energy from sunlight and plants use this energy to make their own food in a process called photosynthesis.

Chromatography A way of separating substances by passing them slowly through an absorbant material.

Circuit A pathway for electricity. A circuit has to be complete for electricity to flow. A switch is a break or a gap in a circuit.

Compressed air Air that has been squashed or compressed into a small space.

Conductor A material such as copper which allows electricity to flow through it easily.

Convection The transfer of heat in a liquid or gas by the movement of the liquid or the gas itself.

Density The mass or 'weight' of a substance per unit of volume. (In other words, how heavy something is for its size.)

Drag The **resistance** to movement in water or air.

Dyes Chemical substances used to colour cloth and other materials.

Dynamo A machine that uses movement to produce electricity.

Electric motor A machine that converts electricity into movement.

Electro-magnet An iron rod with coils of wire wrapped around it. When an electric current is passed through the wire, the rod becomes magnetic.

Elevators Flaps on the tail of an aeroplane which can be moved to make the aeroplane climb or dive through the air.

Filter A screen that stops things, such as coloured light, from passing through it.

Germination The moment when a **seed** starts to grow its first shoot, roots and leaves. For germination to take place, the seed needs the right amount of warmth, moisture and **oxygen**.

Girdle scar A series of rings or circles on a twig, marking the spot where the bud scales have fallen off. It shows where the twig starts to grow each year.

Gravity The force of attraction between any two objects that have mass.

(Mass is the amount of matter a body contains.) Gravity pulls everything on Earth down to the ground and gives things their **weight**.

Hurricane A very violent storm that forms over the west Atlantic Ocean. It is called a typhoon in the Far East and a cyclone in Australia.

Insulator A material such as plastic that does not let electricity flow through it easily.

Lift The force pressing up against flying or gliding things to keep them up in the air.

Lodestone A type of rock which is a natural magnet. It contains an iron ore called magnetite.

Magnetic poles The places on a magnet where the magnetic pull is strongest.

Magnetism The invisible pulling force of a magnet on things made of iron or steel.

Materials The substances from which things are made.

Mordant Substance used to 'fix' colouring material on another substance, so that the colours will not run.

Oxygen An invisible gas with no taste or smell which all living things need to stay alive. Oxygen is also needed for things to burn.

Pigment A substance which gives things colour.

Primary colour One of three colours which mix together to produce any other colour. The primary colours of paint are red, yellow and blue. The primary colours of light are red, green and blue.

Prism A solid shape made of a transparent material which is often triangular. The ends are equal and parallel and the sides have parallel edges.

Reflection The way in which rays of light bounce back from a surface.

Resistance The opposition to the flow of an electric current which is measured in ohms. The more resistance a wire has, the less current it carries.

Runner A long, thin stem which grows out from a plant. New plants grow at intervals along the runner.

Seed A reproductive structure consisting of a young plant and a food store wrapped in a protective coat. It is produced by flowering plants and plants with cones. In the right conditions, a seed will grow into a new plant.

Soil erosion The process by which soil is blown away by the wind or washed away by the rain.

Spore A small reproductive cell which can grow into a new plant. Spores are produced by fungi, algae, mosses and ferns. Some spores have tough, protective coats and can survive dry or cold periods.

Streamlined Something with a smooth, slim shape which cuts through air or water easily.

Testa The protective outer covering of a **seed**.

Transparent Something that lets light go straight through it. You can see clearly through transparent materials.

Tuber A rounded swelling at the end of an underground root or shoot which contains stored food. A potato is a tuber.

Voltage The force which pushes electricity along wires. The higher the voltage, the bigger the electric current.

Weight The force exerted on objects by the pull of **gravity**. Things have weight because gravity pulls them to the ground.

Wind Air moving from place to place. The movement of air causes the weather.

INDEX

Page numbers in
italics refer to
illustrations or where
illustrations and text
occur on the same
page.

Answers to quiz on page 102:
Seeds spread by wind: willowherb, poppy,
thistle. Seeds spread by animals: nut,
blackberry, burdock. Seeds spread by
water: coconut.

The publishers wish to thank the following
artists for contributing to this book:
Peter Bull: page headings, pp.22/23, 24/25,
26/27, 29, 34, 38/39, 54/55, 56/57, 63,
70/71, 80, 84/85, 90–127, 136/137, 142,
154/155, 160/161, 162;
Kuo Kang Chen: cover and pp.12/13, 14/15,
32/33, 36/37, 41, 46/47, 52/53, 58/59,
66/67, 74/75, 78/79, 86/87, 100/101,
110/111, 116/117, 118/119, 132/133,
144/145, 148/149, 150/151;
Eleanor Ludgate of Jillian Burgess
Illustrations: pp.92/93, 108, 122/123;
Josephine Martin of Garden Studio:
pp.94/95, 102/103, 104/105, 114/115,
120/121, 126/127;
Patricia Newell of John Martin & Artists Ltd:
pp.96/97, 98/99, 106/107, 112/113,
124/125;
John Scorey: pp.16/17, 18/19, 20/21, 30/31,
42/43, 44/45, 61, 64/65, 68/69, 73, 76,
82/83, 134/135, 138/139, 140/141,
146/147, 152/153, 156/157, 158/159.

The publishers also wish to thank the
following for kindly supplying photographs
for this book:
Page 13 ZEFA; 16 J. Allan Cash; 21 ZEFA;
27 ZEFA; 28 Frank Lane Picture Agency;
33 Life Agency; 40 Boeing; 42 Life Science
Images; 45 Ministry of Defence; 47 Swift
Picture Library; 53 ZEFA; 60 ZEFA;
62 French Government Tourist Office;
64 J. Allan Cash Photo Library; 65 Dylon;
70 The Guardian (top), ZEFA (bottom);
72 ZEFA; 77 ZEFA; 81 ZEFA; 85 NASA;
87 Biofotos; 92 ZEFA; 103 Frank Lane
Picture Agency; 107 ZEFA; 109 Nature
Photographers; 112 NHPA/Stephen Dalton;
117 NHPA/David Woodfall; 130 Heather
Angel/Biofotos; 123 NHPA/Silvestris;
125 Mark Edwards/Still Pictures; 133 ZEFA;
135 Science Photo Library; 137 Ron
Boardman; 143 ZEFA; 144 National Grid
Company; 149 Science Photo Library;
156 IMITOR; 163 Chris Howes; 165 Science
Photo Library; 166 ZEFA.